Generals killed at Gettysburg

Battle summary included

Editor: Joe Mieczkowski, Licensed Battlefield Guide, Gettysburg NMP

Title: Generals killed at Gettysburg

Subtitle: Battle summary included

Editor: Joe Mieczkowski, Licensed Battlefield Guide, Gettysburg NMP

Created on: 2020-01-23 14:10 (UTC)

ISBN: 978-3-86898-011-0

Produced by: PediaPress GmbH, Moritz-Hilf-Str. 26, Limburg an der Lahn, Germany, http://pediapress.com/

Create your own custom Wikipedia-Book at http://pediapress.com

collection id:
pdf writer version: 0.10.4 mwlib version: 0.16.1

Contents

Introduction

No other battle claimed as many general officers.

This book is about the Battle of Gettysburg and the loss of leadership. Of 120 generals present at Gettysburg, nine were killed or mortally wounded during the battle. The devasting losses sustained among the general officers contributed to the outcome of the battle. Both sides attempted to cope with the death of their leaders and the resulting instability. Following the battle neither army was ever the same again. The South, in particular, never recovered. We can only guess at how the war might have changed had so many not been killed.

The American Civil War was a civil war fought in the United States from 1861 to 1865, between the North and the South. The Civil War began primarily as a result of the long-standing controversy over the enslavement of black people. War broke out in April 1861 when secessionist forces attacked Fort Sumter in South Carolina shortly after Abraham Lincoln had been inaugurated as the President of the United States. The loyalists of the Union in the North proclaimed support for the Constitution. They faced secessionists of the Confederate States in the South, who advocated for states' rights to uphold slavery.

The largest military conflict in North American history began in the summer of 1863 when Union and Confederate forces numbering 160,000 collided at Gettysburg, Pennsylvania. The epic battle lasted three days and resulted in a defeat to Robert E. Lee's Army of Northern Virginia.

Two months prior to Gettysburg, Lee had dealt a stunning defeat to the Army of the Potomac at Chancellorsville, Virginia. He then made plans for a Northern invasion in order to relieve pressure on war-weary Virginia and to seize the initiative from the Yankees. His army, numbering about 75,000, began moving on June 3. The Army of the Potomac, commanded by Joseph Hooker and numbering about 93,000, began moving shortly thereafter, staying between Lee and Washington, D.C. But on June 28, Hooker resigned and was replaced by George G. Meade.

Meade took command of the Army of the Potomac as Lee's army moved into Pennsylvania. On the morning of July 1, advance units of the forces came into contact with one another just outside of Gettysburg. The sound of battle attracted other units, and by noon the conflict was raging. During the first hours of battle, Union General John Reynolds was killed, and the Yankees found that they were outnumbered. The battle lines ran around the northwestern rim of Gettysburg. The Confederates applied pressure all along the Union front, and they slowly drove the Yankees through the town.

By evening, the Federal troops rallied on high ground on the southeastern edge of Gettysburg. As more troops arrived, Meade's army formed a three-mile long, fishhook-shaped line running from Culp's Hill on the right flank, along Cemetery Hill and Cemetery Ridge, to the base of Little Round Top. The Confederates held Gettysburg, and stretched along a six-mile arc around the Union position. Lee's forces would continue to batter each end of the Union position, before launching the infamous Pickett's Charge against the Union center on July 3. The battle concluded when a beaten Lee beat a retreat and returned to Virginia. Lee's army suffered 28,000 casualties (versus Meade's 23,000).

Of 120 generals present at Gettysburg, nine were killed or mortally wounded during the battle. On the Confederate side, generals Semmes, Barksdale, Armistead, Garnett, and Pender (plus Pettigrew during the retreat). On the Union side, generals Reynolds, Zook, Weed, and Farnsworth (and Vincent, promoted posthumously). No other battle claimed as many general officers.

Both armies were badly hurt in the battle. The Union 1st and 3rd Corps never recovered from their casualties and were merged into other corps in March of 1864. Pickett's Division was so badly hurt it was detached from Longstreet and sent to a quiet sector along the Virginia-North Carolina border to recruit and recover. But the Union could more readily find fresh recruits. The consequences for Lee were greater as Lee would increasingly struggle with a shortage of men, particularly of field and general officers.

The rank of general is the highest rank in that branch of the armed services. For that reason, generals serve as the first in the chain of command in the army. Although there were only a handful of generals before the Civil War, by the end of the war more than a thousand men had served as generals. The majority of these generals held other ranks in the military prior to the war and were promoted to general out of a dire need for more commanders to lead the massively expanding Union and Confederate armies. The Civil War counted hundreds of generals on both sides of the Union and Confederate armies, many of whom became very famous. Confederate generals were often former officers of the U.S. Army, but some received the rank by merit. On both sides, the rank of general had to be approved by the president and Senate (of either the Union or Confederate States.) While officers had more prestige than privates, they also carried added burdens, since they were accountable for all the soldiers under their command.

At the outbreak of the Civil War, 296 U.S. Army officers of various grades resigned. Of these, 239 joined the Confederate Army in 1861 and 31 joined after 1861. Of these Confederate officers from the U.S. Army, 184 were United States Military Academy graduates. The other active U.S. Army 809 officers, 640 of whom were West Point graduates, remained with the Union. Of the approximately 900 West Point graduates in civilian life at the beginning of the war, 114 returned to the Union Army and 99 joined the Confederate Army. Norwich University in Northfield, Vermont furnished more officers to the war than any other military school except the United States Military Academy (West Point) and Virginia Military Institute.

Two or more corps would be organized into an army. It is commonly assumed that there was only one army per nation, but in fact both nations had multiple armies in the field

The regiment was the basic maneuver unit of the Civil War. They were recruited from among the eligible citizenry of one or more nearby counties and usually consisted of 1,000 men when first organized. The attrition of disease, combat, and desertion would rapidly reduce this number. Replacements were exceedingly rare for both sides–it was more typical for an entirely new regiment to be raised instead. Regiments were usually led by colonels.

Two or more regiments would be organized into a brigade. Note that it was uncommon for the branches of the army–infantry, cavalry, and artillery–to be mixed within a brigade. A typical brigade would consist of between three and five regiments and be led by a brigadier general.

Two or more brigades would be organized into a division. Divisions tended to be slightly smaller in the Union army–usually two or three brigades. Confederate divisions could include as many as five or six brigades. Divisions were led by major generals.

Two or more divisions would be organized into a corps. A corps typically included infantry, cavalry, and artillery units, the idea being that a corps was a formation that could conduct independent operations.

Two or more corps would be organized into an army. It is commonly assumed that there was only one army per nation, but in fact both nations had multiple armies in the field. The most well-known Confederate armies are the Army of Northern Virginia, led by Robert E. Lee for most of the war, and the Army of Tennessee, which had a string of different commanders. The Union Army of the Potomac was Lee's primary opponent, while the Army of the Cumberland and Army of the Ohio operated out west, among others. At the corps and army level, leadership would usually be determined by seniority among the available major generals, or by intervention from Abraham Lincoln or Confederate President Jefferson Davis.

Duties:

Brigadier General

Commanded infantry or cavalry brigades Combat and administrative duties Positioned regiments in battle Confederate Congress initially made the rank of brigadier general the highest rank Union and Confederate army brigadier generals were similar in assignment Confederate brigadier generals mainly commanded brigades while Union brigadier generals at times would lead divisions as well Often led sub-districts within military departments

Major General

Commanded divisions and led brigade commanders Led districts that made up military departments 88 Confederate men made it to this rank Confederate major generals had to be nominated by Davis and confirmed by the Senate Union major generals led divisions, corps, and entire armies

Lieutenant General

Rank of lieutenant general remained inactive until Winfield Scott received a brevet promotion to the rank in 1855 Unlike the Union, the Confederates promoted numerous officers to the ranks of Lieutenant General and General 18 lieutenant generals in the Confederate Army over the course of the war Confederate lieutenant generals were nominated by Davis and confirmed by the Senate; served as corps commanders Confederate lieutenant general not the same as Union lieutenant general; U.S. Grant and Winfield Scott were the only two Union lieutenant generals

General

Many more appointed Confederate generals than Union generals Outranked all military officers Only seven men achieved the rank of (full) general; the highest ranking was Samuel Cooper, Adjutant General and Inspector General of the Confederate States Army Confederacy: entire army or military department commanders and advisers to Jefferson Davis

Union privates were paid $13 per month until after the final raise of 20 June '64, when they got $16. Pay for one, two, and three-star generals was $315, $457, and $758, respectively. The Confederate pay structure was modeled after that of the US Army. Privates continued to be paid at the prewar rate of $11 per month until June 1864, when the pay of all enlisted men was raised $7 per month. Confederate officer's pay was a few dollars lower than that of their Union counterparts. A Southern B.G for example, drew $301 instead of $315 per month.

Approximately 620,000 soldiers died from combat, accident, starvation, and disease during the Civil War. This number comes from an 1889 study of the war performed by William F. Fox and Thomas Leonard Livermore. Both men fought for the Union. Their estimate is derived from an exhaustive study of the combat and casualty records generated by the armies over five years of fighting.

More than 400 Confederate and 580 Union soldiers advanced to the rank of general during the course of the Civil War, and more than 1 in 10 would die.

A total of 124 generals died–78 for the South and 46 for the North. Officers were often mounted and thus conspicuous targets, none so more than General Officers who often led from the front. Confederate General Stonewall Jackson once said, "Shoot the brave officers, and the cowards will run away and take the men with them."

Robert Selden Garnett was a career military officer, serving in the United States Army until the American Civil War, when he became a Confederate States Army brigadier general. He was the first general officer killed in the Civil War on July 13,1861. He was killed at the Battle of Corrick's Ford in western Virginia (now the state of West Virginia). Nathaniel Lyon was the first Union general to be killed in the American Civil War and is noted for his actions in the state of Missouri. He died on August 10,1861. He was killed at the Battle of Wilson's Creek.

Albert Sidney Johnston was the highest-ranking fatality of the war on either side. He was killed at the Battle of Shiloh. His mortal wound on April 6, 1862, was a strong blow to the morale of the Confederacy. John Sedgwick was killed by a sharpshooter at the Battle of Spotsylvania Court House on May 9, 1864, making him and Major Generals James B. McPherson, Joseph K. Mansfield, and John F. Reynolds the highest-ranking Union soldiers to be killed in the war. Although Major General James B. McPherson was in command of an army at the time of his death and Sedgwick of a corps, Sedgwick had the most senior rank by date of all major generals killed.

Joe Mieczkowski is a retired Federal Executive and a Licensed Battlefield Guide for the Gettysburg National Military Park. Joe is a Past President of The Association of Licensed Battlefield Guides and The Gettysburg Civil War Roundtable. In addition, Joe is on the faculty of the Lincoln Leadership Institute in Gettysburg, PA. He has three books to his credit including "After Gettysburg: Lee retreats and Meade pursues." Joe has been a featured author on C-Span and for The Civil War News.

https://www.history.com/this-day-in-history/the-battle-of-gettysburg-begins   https://www.ncmuseumofhistory.org/civil-war-army-organization-and-rank   https://www.battlefields.org/learn/articles/civil-war-army-organization   http://civil-war-officers.leadr.msu.edu/2015/04/15/chain-of-command-2/

The Battle of Gettysburg

Battle of Gettysburg

```
<indicator name="pp-default"> 🔒 </indicator> <indicator name="pp-default"> 🔒 </indicator> <templatestyles src="Module:Infobox military conflict/styles.css"></templatestyles>
```

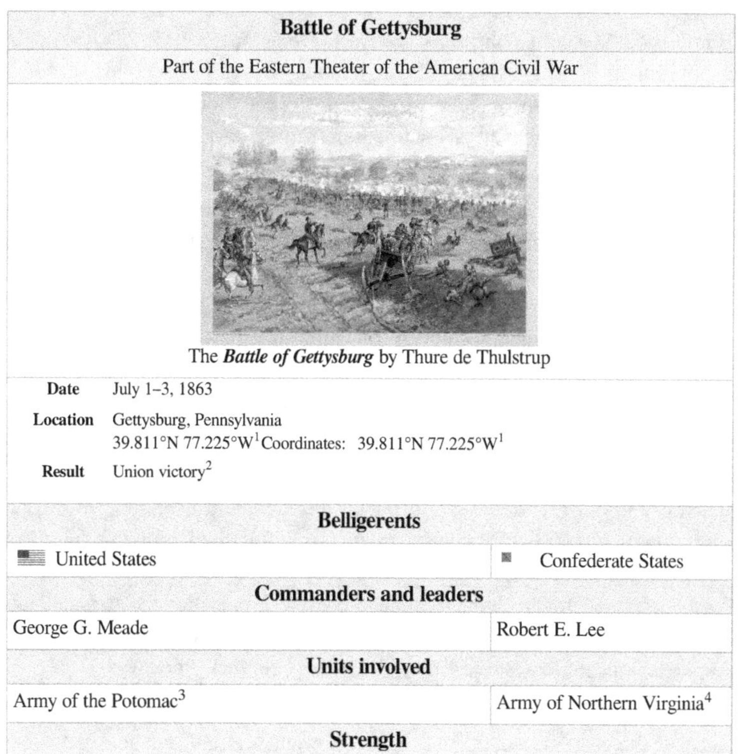

Battle of Gettysburg	
Part of the Eastern Theater of the American Civil War	

The *Battle of Gettysburg* by Thure de Thulstrup

Date	July 1–3, 1863
Location	Gettysburg, Pennsylvania 39.811°N 77.225°W[1] Coordinates: 39.811°N 77.225°W[1]
Result	Union victory[2]

Belligerents	
United States	Confederate States

Commanders and leaders	
George G. Meade	Robert E. Lee

Units involved	
Army of the Potomac[3]	Army of Northern Virginia[4]

Strength	

104,256 ("present for duty")[5,6]	71,000–75,000 (estimated)[7]
Casualties and losses	
23,049 total (3,155 killed; 14,529 wounded; 5,365 captured/missing) 8,9	**23,000–28,000** (estimated)[10,11]

The **Battle of Gettysburg** (locally /ˈɡɛtɪsbɜːrɡ/ (◀ listen))[12] was fought July 1–3, 1863, in and around the town of Gettysburg, Pennsylvania, by Union and Confederate forces during the American Civil War. The battle involved the largest number of casualties of the entire war and is often described as the war's turning point.[13,14] Union Maj. Gen. George Meade's Army of the Potomac defeated attacks by Confederate Gen. Robert E. Lee's Army of Northern Virginia, halting Lee's invasion of the North.

After his success at Chancellorsville in Virginia in May 1863, Lee led his army through the Shenandoah Valley to begin his second invasion of the North—the Gettysburg Campaign. With his army in high spirits, Lee intended to shift the focus of the summer campaign from war-ravaged northern Virginia and hoped to influence Northern politicians to give up their prosecution of the war by penetrating as far as Harrisburg, Pennsylvania, or even Philadelphia. Prodded by President Abraham Lincoln, Maj. Gen. Joseph Hooker moved his army in pursuit, but was relieved of command just three days before the battle and replaced by Meade.

Elements of the two armies initially collided at Gettysburg on July 1, 1863, as Lee urgently concentrated his forces there, his objective being to engage the Union army and destroy it. Low ridges to the northwest of town were defended initially by a Union cavalry division under Brig. Gen. John Buford, and soon reinforced with two corps of Union infantry. However, two large Confederate corps assaulted them from the northwest and north, collapsing the hastily developed Union lines, sending the defenders retreating through the streets of the town to the hills just to the south.

On the second day of battle, most of both armies had assembled. The Union line was laid out in a defensive formation resembling a fishhook. In the late afternoon of July 2, Lee launched a heavy assault on the Union left flank, and fierce fighting raged at Little Round Top, the Wheatfield, Devil's Den, and the Peach Orchard. On the Union right, Confederate demonstrations escalated into full-scale assaults on Culp's Hill and Cemetery Hill. All across the battlefield, despite significant losses, the Union defenders held their lines.

On the third day of battle, fighting resumed on Culp's Hill, and cavalry battles raged to the east and south, but the main event was a dramatic infantry assault by 12,500 Confederates against the center of the Union line on Cemetery

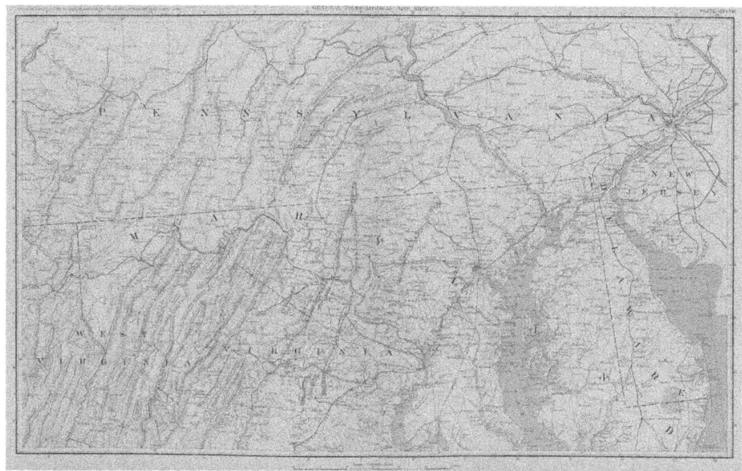

Figure 1: *Northern Virginia, Maryland and Pennsylvania (1861–1865)*

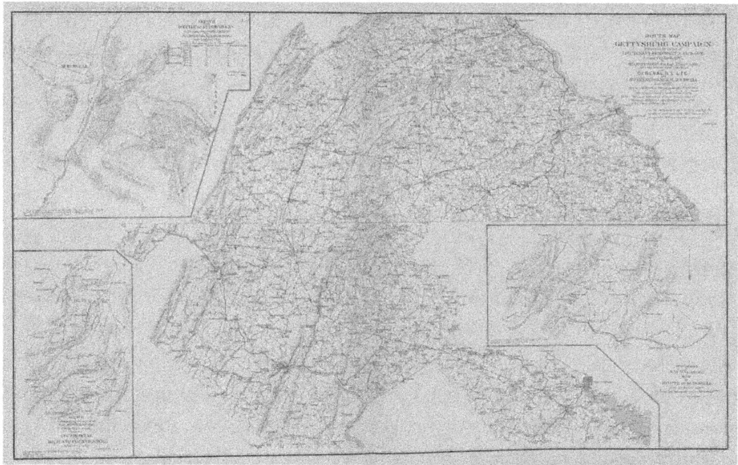

Figure 2: *Gettysburg Campaign, (1863)*

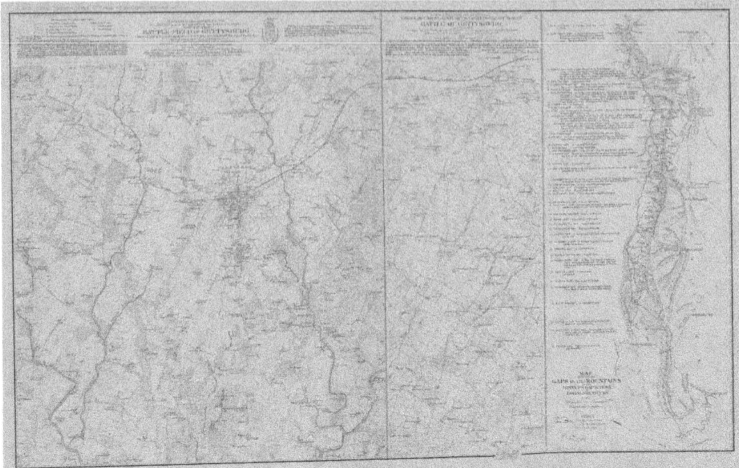

Figure 3: *Battlefield of Gettysburg, (1863)*

Ridge, known as Pickett's Charge. The charge was repulsed by Union rifle and artillery fire, at great loss to the Confederate army.

Lee led his army on a torturous retreat back to Virginia. Between 46,000 and 51,000 soldiers from both armies were casualties in the three-day battle, the most costly in US history.

On November 19, President Lincoln used the dedication ceremony for the Gettysburg National Cemetery to honor the fallen Union soldiers and redefine the purpose of the war in his historic Gettysburg Address.

Background

Military situation

Shortly after the Army of Northern Virginia won a major victory over the Army of the Potomac at the Battle of Chancellorsville (April 30 – May 6, 1863), Robert E. Lee decided upon a second invasion of the North (the first was the unsuccessful Maryland Campaign of September 1862, which ended in the bloody Battle of Antietam). Such a move would upset the Union's plans for the summer campaigning season and possibly reduce the pressure on the besieged Confederate garrison at Vicksburg. The invasion would allow the Confederates to live off the bounty of the rich Northern farms while giving war-ravaged Virginia a much-needed rest. In addition, Lee's 72,000-man army could threaten Philadelphia, Baltimore, and Washington, and possibly strengthen the growing peace movement in the North.[16]

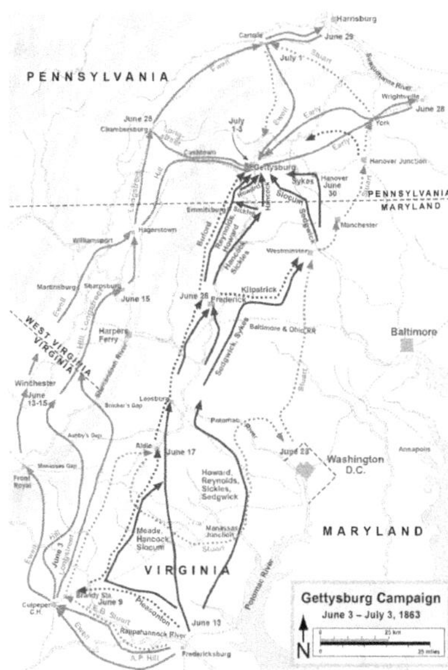

Figure 4:

Gettysburg Campaign (through July 3); cavalry movements shown with dashed lines
Confederate
Union

Initial movements to battle

Thus, on June 3, Lee's army began to shift northward from Fredericksburg, Virginia. Following the death of Thomas J. "Stonewall" Jackson, Lee reorganized his two large corps into three new corps, commanded by Lt. Gen. James Longstreet (First Corps), Lt. Gen. Richard S. Ewell (Second), and Lt. Gen. A.P. Hill (Third); both Ewell and Hill, who had formerly reported to Jackson as division commanders, were new to this level of responsibility. The Cavalry Division remained under the command of Maj. Gen. J.E.B. Stuart.[17]

The Union Army of the Potomac, under Maj. Gen. Joseph Hooker, consisted of seven infantry corps, a cavalry corps, and an Artillery Reserve, for a combined strength of more than 100,000 men.

The first major action of the campaign took place on June 9 between cavalry forces at Brandy Station, near Culpeper, Virginia. The 9,500 Confederate cavalrymen under Stuart were surprised by Maj. Gen. Alfred Pleasonton's combined arms force of two cavalry divisions (8,000 troopers) and 3,000 infantry, but Stuart eventually repulsed the Union attack. The inconclusive battle, the

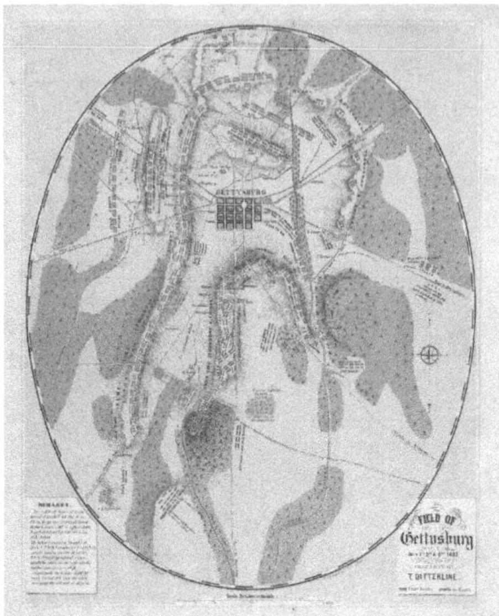

Figure 5: *This 1863 oval-shaped map depicts Gettysburg Battle-field during July 1–3, 1863, showing troop and artillery positions and movements, relief hachures, drainage, roads, railroads, and houses with the names of residents at the time of the Battle of Gettysburg.*

largest predominantly cavalry engagement of the war, proved for the first time that the Union horse soldier was equal to his Southern counterpart.[18]

By mid-June, the Army of Northern Virginia was poised to cross the Potomac River and enter Maryland. After defeating the Union garrisons at Winchester and Martinsburg, Ewell's Second Corps began crossing the river on June 15. Hill's and Longstreet's corps followed on June 24 and 25. Hooker's army pursued, keeping between Washington, D.C. and Lee's army. The Union army crossed the Potomac from June 25 to 27.[19]

Lee gave strict orders for his army to minimize any negative impacts on the civilian population. Food, horses, and other supplies were generally not seized outright, although quartermasters reimbursing Northern farmers and merchants with Confederate money were not well received. Various towns, most notably York, Pennsylvania, were required to pay indemnities in lieu of supplies, under threat of destruction. During the invasion, the Confederates seized some 40 northern African Americans. A few of them were escaped fugitive slaves, but most were freemen; all were sent south into slavery under guard.

Figure 6: *A Harper's Weekly illustration showing Confederate troops escorting captured African American civilians south into slavery. En route to Gettysburg, the Army of Northern Virginia kidnapped approximately 40 black civilians and sent them south into slavery.*[15]

On June 26, elements of Maj. Gen. Jubal Early's division of Ewell's Corps occupied the town of Gettysburg after chasing off newly raised Pennsylvania militia in a series of minor skirmishes. Early laid the borough under tribute, but did not collect any significant supplies. Soldiers burned several railroad cars and a covered bridge, and destroyed nearby rails and telegraph lines. The following morning, Early departed for adjacent York County.[20]

Meanwhile, in a controversial move, Lee allowed J.E.B. Stuart to take a portion of the army's cavalry and ride around the east flank of the Union army. Lee's orders gave Stuart much latitude, and both generals share the blame for the long absence of Stuart's cavalry, as well as for the failure to assign a more active role to the cavalry left with the army. Stuart and his three best brigades were absent from the army during the crucial phase of the approach to Gettysburg and the first two days of battle. By June 29, Lee's army was strung out in an arc from Chambersburg (28 miles (45 km) northwest of Gettysburg) to Carlisle (30 miles (48 km) north of Gettysburg) to near Harrisburg and Wrightsville on the Susquehanna River.[21]

In a dispute over the use of the forces defending the Harpers Ferry garrison, Hooker offered his resignation, and Abraham Lincoln and General-in-Chief

Henry W. Halleck, who were looking for an excuse to rid themselves of him, immediately accepted. They replaced Hooker early on the morning of June 28 with Maj. Gen. George Gordon Meade, then commander of the V Corps.[22]

On June 29, when Lee learned that the Army of the Potomac had crossed the Potomac River, he ordered a concentration of his forces around Cashtown, located at the eastern base of South Mountain and eight miles (13 km) west of Gettysburg.[23] On June 30, while part of Hill's Corps was in Cashtown, one of Hill's brigades, North Carolinians under Brig. Gen. J. Johnston Pettigrew, ventured toward Gettysburg. In his memoirs, Maj. Gen. Henry Heth, Pettigrew's division commander, claimed that he sent Pettigrew to search for supplies in town—especially shoes.[24]

When Pettigrew's troops approached Gettysburg on June 30, they noticed Union cavalry under Brig. Gen. John Buford arriving south of town, and Pettigrew returned to Cashtown without engaging them. When Pettigrew told Hill and Heth what he had seen, neither general believed that there was a substantial Union force in or near the town, suspecting that it had been only Pennsylvania militia. Despite General Lee's order to avoid a general engagement until his entire army was concentrated, Hill decided to mount a significant reconnaissance in force the following morning to determine the size and strength of the enemy force in his front. Around 5 a.m. on Wednesday, July 1, two brigades of Heth's division advanced to Gettysburg.[25]

Opposing forces

Union

> Key commanders (**Army of the Potomac**)

Figure 7:
Maj. Gen.
*George Meade, (**Commanding**) USA*

Figure 8:
Maj. Gen.
John F. Reynolds, USA

Figure 9:
Maj. Gen.
Winfield Scott Hancock, USA

Figure 10:
Maj. Gen.
Daniel Sickles, USA

Figure 11:
Maj. Gen.
George Sykes, USA

Figure 12:
Maj. Gen.
John Sedgwick, USA

Figure 13:
Maj. Gen.
Oliver Otis Howard, USA

Figure 14:
Maj. Gen.
Henry Warner Slocum, USA

Figure 15:
Maj. Gen.
Alfred Pleasonton, USA

The **Army of the Potomac**, initially under Maj. Gen. Joseph Hooker (Maj. Gen. George Meade replaced Hooker in command on June 28), consisted of more than 100,000 men in the following organization:[26]

- I Corps, commanded by Maj. Gen. John F. Reynolds, with divisions commanded by Brig. Gen. James S. Wadsworth, Brig. Gen. John C. Robinson, and Maj. Gen. Abner Doubleday.
- II Corps, commanded by Maj. Gen. Winfield Scott Hancock, with divisions commanded by Brig. Gens. John C. Caldwell, John Gibbon, and Alexander Hays.
- III Corps, commanded by Maj. Gen. Daniel Sickles, with divisions commanded by Maj. Gen. David B. Birney and Maj. Gen. Andrew A. Humphreys.
- V Corps, commanded by Maj. Gen. George Sykes (George G. Meade until June 28), with divisions commanded by Brig. Gens. James Barnes, Romeyn B. Ayres, and Samuel W. Crawford.
- VI Corps, commanded by Maj. Gen. John Sedgwick, with divisions commanded by Brig. Gen. Horatio G. Wright, Brig. Gen. Albion P. Howe, and Maj. Gen. John Newton.
- XI Corps, commanded by Maj. Gen. Oliver Otis Howard, with divisions commanded by Brig. Gen. Francis C. Barlow, Brig. Gen. Adolph von Steinwehr, and Maj. Gen. Carl Schurz.
- XII Corps, commanded by Maj. Gen. Henry W. Slocum, with divisions commanded by Brig. Gens. Alpheus S. Williams and John W. Geary.
- Cavalry Corps, commanded by Maj. Gen. Alfred Pleasonton, with divisions commanded by Brig. Gens. John Buford, David McM. Gregg, and H. Judson Kilpatrick.
- Artillery Reserve, commanded by Brig. Gen. Robert O. Tyler. (The preeminent artillery officer at Gettysburg was Brig. Gen. Henry J. Hunt, chief of artillery on Meade's staff.)

During the advance on Gettysburg, Maj. Gen. Reynolds was in operational command of the left, or advanced, wing of the Army, consisting of the I, III, and XI Corps.[27] Note that many other Union units (not part of the Army of the Potomac) were actively involved in the Gettysburg Campaign, but not directly involved in the Battle of Gettysburg. These included portions of the Union IV Corps, the militia and state troops of the Department of the Susquehanna, and various garrisons, including that at Harpers Ferry.

Confederate

Key commanders (**Army of Northern Virginia**)

Figure 16:
Gen.
*Robert E. Lee, (**Commanding**) CSA*

Figure 17:
Lt. Gen.
James Longstreet, CSA

Figure 18:
Lt.. Gen.
Richard S. Ewell, CSA

Figure 19:
Lt. Gen.
A. P. Hill, CSA

Figure 20:
Maj. Gen.
J.E.B. Stuart, CSA

In reaction to the death of Lt. Gen. Thomas J. "Stonewall" Jackson after Chancellorsville, Lee reorganized his **Army of Northern Virginia** (75,000 men) from two infantry corps into three.[28]

- First Corps, commanded by Lt. Gen. James Longstreet, with divisions commanded by Maj. Gens. Lafayette McLaws, George Pickett, and John Bell Hood.
- Second Corps, commanded by Lt. Gen. Richard S. Ewell, with divisions commanded by Maj. Gens. Jubal A. Early, Edward "Allegheny" Johnson, and Robert E. Rodes.
- Third Corps, commanded by Lt. Gen. A.P. Hill, with divisions commanded by Maj. Gens. Richard H. Anderson, Henry Heth, and W. Dorsey Pender.
- Cavalry division, commanded by Maj. Gen. J.E.B. Stuart, with brigades commanded by Brig. Gens. Wade Hampton, Fitzhugh Lee, Beverly H. Robertson, Albert G. Jenkins, William E. "Grumble" Jones, and John D. Imboden, and Col. John R. Chambliss.

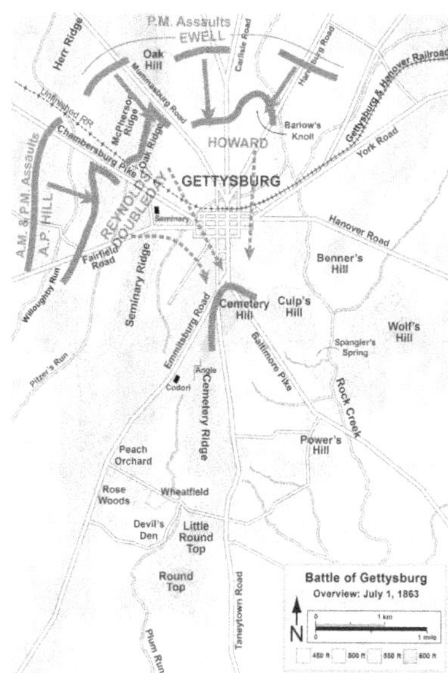

Figure 21: *Overview map of the first day of the Battle of Gettysburg, July 1, 1863*

First day of battle

Herr Ridge, McPherson Ridge and Seminary Ridge

Anticipating that the Confederates would march on Gettysburg from the west on the morning of July 1, Buford laid out his defenses on three ridges west of the town: **Herr Ridge**, **McPherson Ridge** and **Seminary Ridge**. These were appropriate terrain for a delaying action by his small cavalry division against superior Confederate infantry forces, meant to buy time awaiting the arrival of Union infantrymen who could occupy the strong defensive positions south of town at Cemetery Hill, Cemetery Ridge, and Culp's Hill. Buford understood that if the Confederates could gain control of these heights, Meade's army would have difficulty dislodging them.[29]

Confederate General Henry Heth's division advanced with two brigades forward, commanded by Brig. Gens. James J. Archer and Joseph R. Davis. They proceeded easterly in columns along the Chambersburg Pike. Three miles (5 km) west of town, about 7:30 a.m. on July 1, the two brigades met light resistance from vedettes of Union cavalry, and deployed into line. According to lore, the Union soldier to fire the first shot of the battle was Lt. Marcellus Jones. Lt. Jones later returned to Gettysburg, in 1886 erecting a monument marking the spot where he fired the first shot. Eventually, Heth's men reached

Figure 22: *First shot monument*

dismounted troopers of Col. William Gamble's cavalry brigade, who raised determined resistance and delaying tactics from behind fence posts with fire from their breechloading carbines.[30] Still, by 10:20 a.m., the Confederates had pushed the Union cavalrymen east to McPherson Ridge, when the vanguard of the I Corps (Maj. Gen. John F. Reynolds) finally arrived.[31]

North of the pike, Davis gained a temporary success against Brig. Gen. Lysander Cutler's brigade but was repulsed with heavy losses in an action around an unfinished railroad bed cut in the ridge. South of the pike, Archer's brigade assaulted through Herbst (also known as McPherson's) Woods. The Union Iron Brigade under Brig. Gen. Solomon Meredith enjoyed initial success against Archer, capturing several hundred men, including Archer himself.[32]

General Reynolds was shot and killed early in the fighting while directing troop and artillery placements just to the east of the woods. Shelby Foote wrote that the Union cause lost a man considered by many to be "the best general in the army."[33] Maj. Gen. Abner Doubleday assumed command. Fighting in the Chambersburg Pike area lasted until about 12:30 p.m. It resumed around 2:30 p.m., when Heth's entire division engaged, adding the brigades of Pettigrew and Col. John M. Brockenbrough.[34]

As Pettigrew's North Carolina Brigade came on line, they flanked the 19th Indiana and drove the Iron Brigade back. The 26th North Carolina (the largest regiment in the army with 839 men) lost heavily, leaving the first day's fight with around 212 men. By the end of the three-day battle, they had about 152 men standing, the highest casualty percentage for one battle of any regiment, North or South.[35] Slowly the Iron Brigade was pushed out of the woods toward Seminary Ridge. Hill added Maj. Gen. William Dorsey Pender's division to the assault, and the I Corps was driven back through the grounds of the Lutheran Seminary and Gettysburg streets.[36]

As the fighting to the west proceeded, two divisions of Ewell's Second Corps, marching west toward Cashtown in accordance with Lee's order for the army to concentrate in that vicinity, turned south on the Carlisle and Harrisburg roads toward Gettysburg, while the Union XI Corps (Maj. Gen. Oliver O. Howard) raced north on the Baltimore Pike and Taneytown Road. By early afternoon, the Union line ran in a semicircle west, north, and northeast of Gettysburg.[37]

However, the Union did not have enough troops; Cutler, whose brigade was deployed north of the Chambersburg Pike, had his right flank in the air. The leftmost division of the XI Corps was unable to deploy in time to strengthen the line, so Doubleday was forced to throw in reserve brigades to salvage his line.[38]

Around 2 p.m., the Confederate Second Corps divisions of Maj. Gens. Robert E. Rodes and Jubal Early assaulted and out-flanked the Union I and XI Corps positions north and northwest of town. The Confederate brigades of Col. Edward A. O'Neal and Brig. Gen. Alfred Iverson suffered severe losses assaulting the I Corps division of Brig. Gen. John C. Robinson south of Oak Hill. Early's division profited from a blunder by Brig. Gen. Francis C. Barlow, when he advanced his XI Corps division to Blocher's Knoll (directly north of town and now known as Barlow's Knoll); this represented a salient[39] in the corps line, susceptible to attack from multiple sides, and Early's troops overran Barlow's division, which constituted the right flank of the Union Army's position. Barlow was wounded and captured in the attack.[40]

As Union positions collapsed both north and west of town, Gen. Howard ordered a retreat to the high ground south of town at Cemetery Hill, where he had left the division of Brig. Gen. Adolph von Steinwehr in reserve.[41] Maj. Gen. Winfield S. Hancock assumed command of the battlefield, sent by Meade when he heard that Reynolds had been killed. Hancock, commander of the II Corps and Meade's most trusted subordinate, was ordered to take command of the field and to determine whether Gettysburg was an appropriate place for a major battle.[42] Hancock told Howard, "I think this the strongest position by nature upon which to fight a battle that I ever saw." When Howard agreed, Hancock concluded the discussion: "Very well, sir, I select this as the battlefield." Hancock's determination had a morale-boosting effect on the retreating Union soldiers, but he played no direct tactical role on the first day.[43]

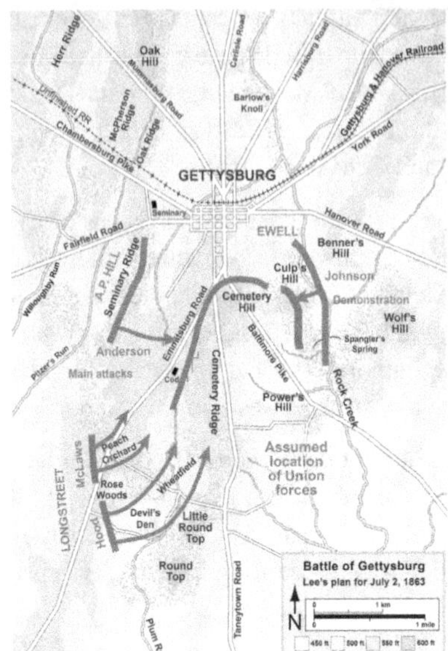

Figure 23: *Robert E. Lee's plan for July 2, 1863*

General Lee understood the defensive potential to the Union if they held this high ground. He sent orders to Ewell that Cemetery Hill be taken "if practicable." Ewell, who had previously served under Stonewall Jackson, a general well known for issuing peremptory orders, determined such an assault was not practicable and, thus, did not attempt it; this decision is considered by historians to be a great missed opportunity.[44]

The first day at Gettysburg, more significant than simply a prelude to the bloody second and third days, ranks as the 23rd biggest battle of the war by number of troops engaged. About one quarter of Meade's army (22,000 men) and one third of Lee's army (27,000) were engaged.[45]

Second day of battle

Plans and movement to battle

Throughout the evening of July 1 and morning of July 2, most of the remaining infantry of both armies arrived on the field, including the Union II, III, V, VI, and XII Corps. Two of Longstreet's divisions were on the road: Brig. Gen. George Pickett, had begun the 22 mile (35 km) march from Chambersburg, while Brig. Gen. E. M. Law had begun the march from Guilford. Both arrived late in the morning. Law completed his 28-mile (45 km) march in eleven hours.[46]

The Union line ran from Culp's Hill southeast of the town, northwest to Cemetery Hill just south of town, then south for nearly two miles (3 km) along Cemetery Ridge, terminating just north of Little Round Top. Most of the XII Corps was on Culp's Hill; the remnants of I and XI Corps defended Cemetery Hill; II Corps covered most of the northern half of Cemetery Ridge; and III Corps was ordered to take up a position to its flank. The shape of the Union line is popularly described as a "fishhook" formation.

The Confederate line paralleled the Union line about a mile (1,600 m) to the west on Seminary Ridge, ran east through the town, then curved southeast to a point opposite Culp's Hill. Thus, the Union army had interior lines, while the Confederate line was nearly five miles (8 km) long.[47]

Lee's battle plan for July 2 called for a general assault of Meade's positions. On the right, Longstreet's First Corps was to position itself to attack the Union left flank, facing northeast astraddle the Emmitsburg Road, and to roll up the Union line. The attack sequence was to begin with Maj. Gens. John Bell Hood's and Lafayette McLaws's divisions, followed by Maj. Gen. Richard H. Anderson's division of Hill's Third Corps.[48]

On the left, Lee instructed Ewell to position his Second Corps to attack Culp's Hill and Cemetery Hill when he heard the gunfire from Longstreet's assault, preventing Meade from shifting troops to bolster his left. Though it does not appear in either his or Lee's Official Report, Ewell claimed years later that Lee had changed the order to simultaneously attack, calling for only a "diversion", to be turned into a full-scale attack if a favorable opportunity presented itself.[49,50]

Lee's plan, however, was based on faulty intelligence, exacerbated by Stuart's continued absence from the battlefield. Though Lee personally reconnoitered his left during the morning, he did not visit Longstreet's position on the Confederate right. Even so, Lee rejected suggestions that Longstreet move beyond Meade's left and attack the Union flank, capturing the supply trains and effectively blocking Meade's escape route.[51]

Lee did not issue orders for the attack until 11:00 a.m.[52] About noon, General Anderson's advancing troops were discovered by General Sickles' outpost guard and the Third Corps–upon which Longstreet's First Corps was to form–did not get into position until 1:00 p.m.[53]

Hood and McLaws, after their long march, were not yet in position and did not launch their attacks until just after 4 p.m. and 5 p.m., respectively.[54]

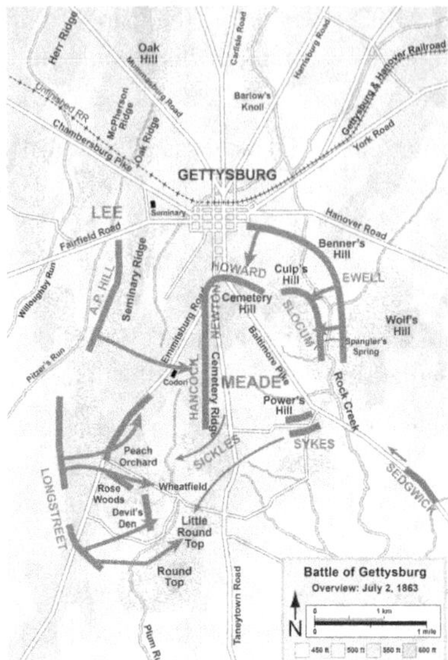

Figure 24: *Overview map of the second day*
of the Battle of Gettysburg, July 2, 1863

Attacks on the Union left flank

As Longstreet's left division, under Maj. Gen. Lafayette McLaws, advanced,
they unexpectedly found Maj. Gen. Daniel Sickles's III Corps directly in their
path. Sickles had been dissatisfied with the position assigned him on the southern end of Cemetery Ridge. Seeing ground better suited for artillery positions
a half mile (800 m) to the west— centered at the Sherfy farm's Peach Orchard—he violated orders and advanced his corp to the slightly higher ground
along the Emmitsburg Road, moving away from Cemetery Ridge. The new
line ran from Devil's Den, northwest to the Peach Orchard, then northeast
along the Emmitsburg Road to south of the Codori farm. This created an
untenable salient at the Peach Orchard; Brig. Gen. Andrew A. Humphreys's
division (in position along the Emmitsburg Road) and Maj. Gen. David B. Birney's division (to the south) were subject to attacks from two sides and were
spread out over a longer front than their small corps could defend effectively.[55]
The Confederate artillery was ordered to open fire at 3:00 p.m.[56] After failing
to attend a meeting at this time of Meade's corps commanders, Meade rode
to Sickles' position and demanded an explanation of the situation. Knowing a
Confederate attack was imminent and a retreat would be endangered, Meade
refused Sickles' offer to withdraw.[57]

Meade was forced to send 20,000 reinforcements:[58] the entire V Corps, Brig. Gen. John C. Caldwell's division of the II Corps, most of the XII Corps, and portions of the newly arrived VI Corps. Hood's division moved more to the east than intended, losing its alignment with the Emmitsburg Road,[59] attacking Devil's Den and Little Round Top. McLaws, coming in on Hood's left, drove multiple attacks into the thinly stretched III Corps in the Wheatfield and overwhelmed them in Sherfy's Peach Orchard. McLaws's attack eventually reached Plum Run Valley (the "Valley of Death") before being beaten back by the Pennsylvania Reserves division of the V Corps, moving down from Little Round Top. The III Corps was virtually destroyed as a combat unit in this battle, and Sickles's leg was amputated after it was shattered by a cannonball. Caldwell's division was destroyed piecemeal in the Wheatfield. Anderson's division, coming from McLaws's left and starting forward around 6 p.m., reached the crest of Cemetery Ridge, but could not hold the position in the face of counterattacks from the II Corps, including an almost suicidal bayonet charge by the 1st Minnesota regiment against a Confederate brigade, ordered in desperation by Hancock to buy time for reinforcements to arrive.[60]

As fighting raged in the Wheatfield and Devil's Den, Col. Strong Vincent of V Corps had a precarious hold on Little Round Top, an important hill at the extreme left of the Union line. His brigade of four relatively small regiments was able to resist repeated assaults by Brig. Gen. Evander M. Law's brigade of Hood's division. Meade's chief engineer, Brig. Gen. Gouverneur K. Warren, had realized the importance of this position, and dispatched Vincent's brigade, an artillery battery, and the 140th New York to occupy Little Round Top mere minutes before Hood's troops arrived. The defense of Little Round Top with a bayonet charge by the 20th Maine, ordered by Col. Joshua L. Chamberlain but possibly led by Lt. Holman S. Melcher, was one of the most fabled episodes in the Civil War and propelled Col. Chamberlain into prominence after the war.[61]

Attacks on the Union right flank

Ewell interpreted his orders as calling only for a cannonade. His 32 guns, along with A. P. Hill's 55 guns, engaged in a two-hour artillery barrage at extreme range that had little effect. Finally, about six o'clock, Ewell sent orders to each of his division commanders to attack the Union lines in his front.

Maj. Gen. Edward "Allegheny" Johnson's Division "had not been pushed close to [Culp's Hill] in preparation for an assault, although one had been contemplated all day. It now had a full mile (1,600 m) to advance and Rock Creek had to be crossed. This could only be done at few places and involved much delay. Only three of Johnson's four brigades moved to the attack."[62] Most of the hill's defenders, the Union XII Corps, had been sent to the left to

Figure 25: *Union breastworks on Culp's Hill*

defend against Longstreet's attacks, leaving only a brigade of New Yorkers under Brig. Gen. George S. Greene behind strong, newly constructed defensive works. With reinforcements from the I and XI Corps, Greene's men held off the Confederate attackers, though giving up some of the lower earthworks on the lower part of Culp's Hill.[63]

Early was similarly unprepared when he ordered Harry T. Hays' and Isaac E. Avery's Brigades to attack the Union XI Corps positions on East Cemetery Hill. Once started, fighting was fierce: Col. Andrew L. Harris of the Union 2nd Brigade, 1st Division, came under a withering attack, losing half his men. Avery was wounded early on, but the Confederates reached the crest of the hill and entered the Union breastworks, capturing one or two batteries. Seeing he was not supported on his right, Hays withdrew. His right was to be supported by Robert E. Rodes' Division, but Rodes—like Early and Johnson—had not been ordered up in preparation for the attack. He had twice as far to travel as Early; by the time he came in contact with the Union skirmish line, Early's troops had already begun to withdraw.[64]

Jeb Stuart and his three cavalry brigades arrived in Gettysburg around noon but had no role in the second day's battle. Brig. Gen. Wade Hampton's brigade fought a minor engagement with newly promoted 23-year-old Brig. Gen. George Armstrong Custer's Michigan cavalry near Hunterstown to the northeast of Gettysburg.[65]

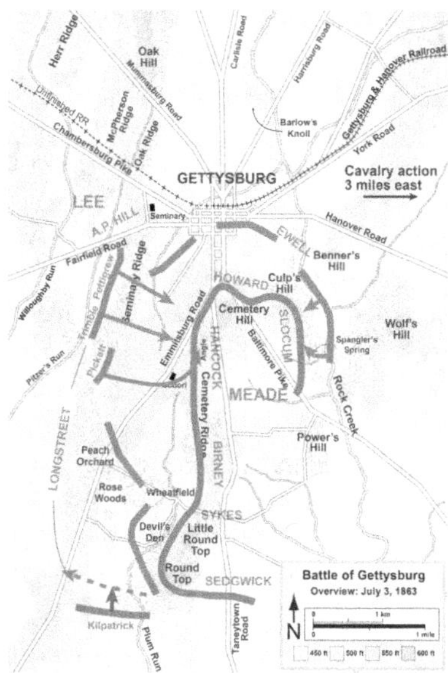

Figure 26: *Overview map of the third day of the Battle of Gettysburg, July 3, 1863*

Third day of battle

Lee's plan

General Lee wished to renew the attack on Friday, July 3, using the same basic plan as the previous day: Longstreet would attack the Union left, while Ewell attacked Culp's Hill.[66] However, before Longstreet was ready, Union XII Corps troops started a dawn artillery bombardment against the Confederates on Culp's Hill in an effort to regain a portion of their lost works. The Confederates attacked, and the second fight for Culp's Hill ended around 11 a.m. Harry Pfanz judged that, after some seven hours of bitter combat, "the Union line was intact and held more strongly than before."[67]

Lee was forced to change his plans. Longstreet would command Pickett's Virginia division of his own First Corps, plus six brigades from Hill's Corps, in an attack on the Union II Corps position at the right center of the Union line on Cemetery Ridge. Prior to the attack, all the artillery the Confederacy could bring to bear on the Union positions would bombard and weaken the enemy's line.[68]

Much has been made over the years of General Longstreet's objections to General Lee's plan. In his memoirs, Longstreet described their discussion as follows:

<templatestyles src="Template:Quote/styles.css"/>

> *[Lee] rode over after sunrise and gave his orders. His plan was to as-sault the enemy's left centre by a column to be composed of McLaws's and Hood's divisions reinforced by Pickett's brigades. I thought that it would not do; that the point had been fully tested the day before, by more men, when all were fresh; that the enemy was there looking for us, as we heard him during the night putting up his defences; that the divisions of McLaws and Hood were holding a mile [1,600 m] along the right of my line against twenty thousand men, who would follow their withdrawal, strike the flank of the assaulting column, crush it, and get on our rear towards the Potomac River; that thirty thousand men was the minimum of force necessary for the work; that even such force would need close co-operation on other parts of the line; that the column as he proposed to organize it would have only about thirteen thousand men (the divisions having lost a third of their numbers the day before); that the column would have to march a mile [1,600 m] under concentrating battery fire, and a thousand yards [900 m] under long-range musketry; that the conditions were different from those in the days of Napoleon, when field batteries had a range of six hundred yards [550 m] and musketry about sixty yards [55 m].*
>
> *He said the distance was not more than fourteen hundred yards [1280 m]. General Meade's estimate was a mile or a mile and a half [1.6 or 2.4 km] (Captain Long, the guide of the field of Gettysburg in 1888, stated that it was a trifle over a mile). He then concluded that the divisions of McLaws and Hood could remain on the defensive line; that he would reinforce by divisions of the Third Corps and Pickett's brigades, and stated the point to which the march should be directed. I asked the strength of the column. He stated fifteen thousand. Opinion was then expressed that the fifteen thousand men who could make successful assault over that field had never been arrayed for battle; but he was impatient of listening, and tired of talking, and nothing was left but to proceed.*[69]

The largest artillery bombardment of the war

Around 1 p.m., from 150 to 170 Confederate guns began an artillery bom-bardment that was probably the largest of the war. In order to save valuable ammunition for the infantry attack that they knew would follow, the Army of the Potomac's artillery, under the command of Brig. Gen. Henry Jackson Hunt, at first did not return the enemy's fire. After waiting about 15 minutes, about 80 Union cannons added to the din. The Army of Northern Virginia was critically low on artillery ammunition, and the cannonade did not significantly affect the Union position.[70]

Figure 27: *The "High Water Mark" on Cemetery Ridge as it appears today. The monument to the 72nd Pennsylvania Volunteer Infantry Regiment ("Baxter's Philadelphia Fire Zouaves") appears at right, the Copse of Trees to the left.*

Pickett's Charge

Around 3 p.m., the cannon fire subsided, and 12,500 Southern soldiers stepped from the ridgeline and advanced the three-quarters of a mile (1,200 m) to Cemetery Ridge in what is known to history as "Pickett's Charge". As the Confederates approached, there was fierce flanking artillery fire from Union positions on Cemetery Hill and north of Little Round Top, and musket and canister fire from Hancock's II Corps. In the Union center, the commander of artillery had held fire during the Confederate bombardment (in order to save it for the infantry assault, which Meade had correctly predicted the day before), leading Southern commanders to believe the Northern cannon batteries had been knocked out. However, they opened fire on the Confederate infantry during their approach with devastating results. Nearly one half of the attackers did not return to their own lines.

Although the Union line wavered and broke temporarily at a jog called the "Angle" in a low stone fence, just north of a patch of vegetation called the Copse of Trees, reinforcements rushed into the breach, and the Confederate attack was repulsed. The farthest advance of Brig. Gen. Lewis A. Armistead's brigade of Maj. Gen. George Pickett's division at the Angle is referred to as the "High-water mark of the Confederacy", arguably representing the closest the South ever came to its goal of achieving independence from the

Union via military victory.[71] Union and Confederate soldiers locked in hand-to-hand combat, attacking with their rifles, bayonets, rocks and even their bare hands. Armistead ordered his Confederates to turn two captured cannons against Union troops, but discovered that there was no ammunition left, the last double canister shots having been used against the charging Confederates. Armistead was wounded shortly afterward three times.

Cavalry battles

There were two significant cavalry engagements on July 3. Stuart was sent to guard the Confederate left flank and was to be prepared to exploit any success the infantry might achieve on Cemetery Hill by flanking the Union right and hitting their trains and lines of communications. Three miles (5 km) east of Gettysburg, in what is now called "East Cavalry Field" (not shown on the accompanying map, but between the York and Hanover Roads), Stuart's forces collided with Union cavalry: Brig. Gen. David McMurtrie Gregg's division and Brig. Gen. Custer's brigade. A lengthy mounted battle, including hand-to-hand sabre combat, ensued. Custer's charge, leading the 1st Michigan Cavalry, blunted the attack by Wade Hampton's brigade, blocking Stuart from achieving his objectives in the Union rear.

Meanwhile, after hearing news of the day's victory, Brig. Gen. Judson Kilpatrick launched a cavalry attack against the infantry positions of Longstreet's Corps southwest of Big Round Top. Brig. Gen. Elon J. Farnsworth protested against the futility of such a move, but obeyed orders. Farnsworth was killed in the attack, and his brigade suffered significant losses.[72]

Aftermath

Casualties

The two armies suffered between 46,000 and 51,000 casualties, nearly one third of all total troops engaged, 28% of the Army of the Potomac and 37% of the Army of Northern Virginia.[73] Union casualties were 23,055 (3,155 killed, 14,531 wounded, 5,369 captured or missing), while Confederate casualties are more difficult to estimate. Many authors have referred to as many as 28,000 Confederate casualties,[74] and Busey and Martin's more recent 2005 work, *Regimental Strengths and Losses at Gettysburg*, documents 23,231 (4,708 killed, 12,693 wounded, 5,830 captured or missing). Nearly a third of Lee's general officers were killed, wounded, or captured.[75] The casualties for both sides during the entire campaign were 57,225.[76]

In addition to being the deadliest battle of the war, Gettysburg also had the highest number of generals killed in action. The Confederacy lost generals Paul

Figure 28: *'The Harvest of Death": Union dead on the battlefield at Gettysburg, Pennsylvania, photographed July 5 or July 6, 1863, by Timothy H. O'Sullivan*

Jones Semmes, William Barksdale, William Dorsey Pender, Richard Garnett, and Lewis Armistead, as well as J. Johnston Pettigrew during the retreat after the battle. The Union lost Generals John Reynolds, Samuel K. Zook, Stephen H. Weed, and Elon J. Farnsworth, as well as Strong Vincent, who after being mortally wounded was given a deathbed promotion to brigadier general. Additional senior officer casualties included the wounding of Union Generals Dan Sickles (lost a leg), Francis C. Barlow, Daniel Butterfield, and Winfield Scott Hancock. For the Confederacy, Major General John Bell Hood lost the use of his left arm, while Major General Henry Heth received a shot to the head on the first day of battle (though incapacitated for the rest of the battle, he remarkably survived without long term injuries, credited in part due to his hat stuffed full of paper dispatches). Confederate Generals James L. Kemper and Isaac R. Trimble were severely wounded during Pickett's charge and captured during the Confederate retreat. General James J. Archer, in command of a brigade that most likely was responsible for killing Reynolds, was taken prisoner shortly after Reynolds' death.

The following tables summarize casualties by corps for the Union and Confederate forces during the three-day battle.[77]

Union Corps	Casualties (k/w/m)
I Corps	6059 (666/3231/2162)
II Corps	4369 (797/3194/378)
III Corps	4211 (593/3029/589)
V Corps	2187 (365/1611/211)
VI Corps	242 (27/185/30)
XI Corps	3807 (369/1924/1514)
XII Corps	1082 (204/812/66)
Cavalry Corps	852 (91/354/407)
Artillery Reserve	242 (43/187/12)

Confederate Corps	Casualties (k/w/m)
First Corps	7665 (1617/4205/1843)
Second Corps	6686 (1301/3629/1756)
Third Corps	8495 (1724/4683/2088)
Cavalry Corps	380 (66/174/140)

Bruce Catton wrote, "The town of Gettysburg looked as if some universal moving day had been interrupted by catastrophe."[78] But there was only one documented civilian death during the battle: Ginnie Wade (also widely known as Jennie), 20 years old, was hit by a stray bullet that passed through her kitchen in town while she was making bread.[79] Another notable civilian casualty was John L. Burns, a 69-year old veteran of the War of 1812 who walked to the front lines on the first day of battle and participated in heavy combat as a volunteer, receiving numerous wounds in the process. Despite his age and injuries, Burns survived the battle and lived until 1872. Nearly 8,000 had been killed outright; these bodies, lying in the hot summer sun, needed to be buried quickly. Over 3,000 horse carcasses[80] were burned in a series of piles south of town; townsfolk became violently ill from the stench.[81] Meanwhile, the town of Gettysburg, with its population of just 2,400, found itself tasked with taking care of 14,000 wounded Union troops and an additional 8,000 Confederate prisoners.

Confederate retreat

The armies stared at one another in a heavy rain across the bloody fields on July 4, the same day that, some 900 miles (1,500 km) away, the Vicksburg garrison surrendered to Maj. Gen. Ulysses S. Grant. Lee had reformed his lines into a defensive position on Seminary Ridge the night of July 3, evacuating the

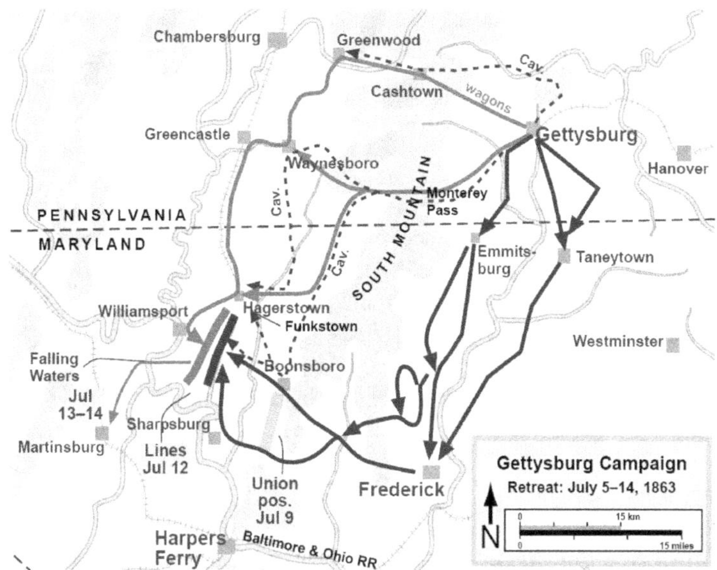

Figure 29: *Gettysburg Campaign (July 5 – July 14, 1863)*

town of Gettysburg. The Confederates remained on the battlefield, hoping that Meade would attack, but the cautious Union commander decided against the risk, a decision for which he would later be criticized. Both armies began to collect their remaining wounded and bury some of the dead. A proposal by Lee for a prisoner exchange was rejected by Meade.[82]

Lee started his Army of Northern Virginia in motion late the evening of July 4 towards Fairfield and Chambersburg. Cavalry under Brig. Gen. John D. Imboden was entrusted to escort the miles-long wagon train of supplies and wounded men that Lee wanted to take back to Virginia with him, using the route through Cashtown and Hagerstown to Williamsport, Maryland. Meade's army followed, although the pursuit was half-spirited. The recently rain-swollen Potomac trapped Lee's army on the north bank of the river for a time, but when the Union troops finally caught up, the Confederates had forded the river. The rear-guard action at Falling Waters on July 14 added some more names to the long casualty lists, including General Pettigrew, who was mortally wounded.[83] General James L. Kemper, severely wounded during Pickett's charge, was captured during Lee's retreat.

In a brief letter to Maj. Gen. Henry W. Halleck written on July 7, Lincoln remarked on the two major Union victories at Gettysburg and Vicksburg. He continued:

```
<templatestyles src="Template:Quote/styles.css"/>
```

> *Now, if Gen. Meade can complete his work so gloriously prosecuted thus far, by the literal or substantial destruction of Lee's army, the rebellion will be over.*[84]

Halleck then relayed the contents of Lincoln's letter to Meade in a telegram. However, the Army of the Potomac was exhausted by days of fighting and heavy losses. Furthermore, Meade was forced to detach 4,000 troops North to suppress the New York City Draft Riots[85], further reducing the effectiveness of his pursuit. Despite repeated pleas from Lincoln and Halleck, which continued over the next week, Meade did not pursue Lee's army aggressively enough to destroy it before it crossed back over the Potomac River to safety in the South. The campaign continued into Virginia with light engagements until July 23, in the minor Battle of Manassas Gap, after which Meade abandoned any attempts at pursuit and the two armies took up positions across from each other on the Rappahannock River.[86]

Union reaction to the news of the victory

The news of the Union victory electrified the North. A headline in *The Philadelphia Inquirer* proclaimed "VICTORY! WATERLOO ECLIPSED!" New York diarist George Templeton Strong wrote:[87]

```
<templatestyles src="Template:Quote/styles.css"/>
```

> *The results of this victory are priceless. ... The charm of Robert E. Lee's invincibility is broken. The Army of the Potomac has at last found a general that can handle it, and has stood nobly up to its terrible work in spite of its long disheartening list of hard-fought failures. ... Copperheads are palsied and dumb for the moment at least. ... Government is strengthened four-fold at home and abroad.*

> —*George Templeton Strong, Diary, p. 330.*

However, the Union enthusiasm soon dissipated as the public realized that Lee's army had escaped destruction and the war would continue. Lincoln complained to Secretary of the Navy Gideon Welles that "Our army held the war in the hollow of their hand and they would not close it!"[88] Brig. Gen. Alexander S. Webb wrote to his father on July 17, stating that such Washington politicians as "Chase, Seward and others," disgusted with Meade, "write to me that Lee really won that Battle!"[89]

Effect on the Confederacy

In fact, the Confederates had lost militarily and also politically. During the final hours of the battle, Confederate Vice President Alexander Stephens was approaching the Union lines at Norfolk, Virginia, under a flag of truce. Although his formal instructions from Confederate President Jefferson Davis had limited his powers to negotiate on prisoner exchanges and other procedural matters, historian James M. McPherson speculates that he had informal goals of presenting peace overtures. Davis had hoped that Stephens would reach Washington from the south while Lee's victorious army was marching toward it from the north. President Lincoln, upon hearing of the Gettysburg results, refused Stephens's request to pass through the lines. Furthermore, when the news reached London, any lingering hopes of European recognition of the Confederacy were finally abandoned. Henry Adams, whose father was serving as the U.S ambassador to the United Kingdom at the time, wrote, "The disasters of the rebels are unredeemed by even any hope of success. It is now conceded that all idea of intervention is at an end."[90]

Compounding the effects of the defeat would be the end of the Siege of Vicksburg, which surrendered to Grant's Federal armies in the West on July 4, the day after the Gettysburg battle.

The immediate reaction of the Southern military and public sectors was that Gettysburg was a setback, not a disaster. The sentiment was that Lee had been successful on July 1 and had fought a valiant battle on July 2–3, but could not dislodge the Union Army from the strong defensive position to which it fled. The Confederates successfully stood their ground on July 4 and withdrew only after they realized Meade would not attack them. The withdrawal to the Potomac that could have been a disaster was handled masterfully. Furthermore, the Army of the Potomac had been kept away from Virginia farmlands for the summer and all predicted that Meade would be too timid to threaten them for the rest of the year. Lee himself had a positive view of the campaign, writing to his wife that the army had returned "rather sooner than I had originally contemplated, but having accomplished what I proposed on leaving the Rappahannock, viz., relieving the Valley of the presence of the enemy and drawing his Army north of the Potomac." He was quoted as saying to Maj. John Seddon, brother of the Confederate secretary of war, "Sir, we did whip them at Gettysburg, and it will be seen for the next six months that *that army* will be as quiet as a sucking dove." Some Southern publications, such as the *Charleston Mercury*, were critical of Lee's actions. On August 8, Lee offered his resignation to President Davis, who quickly rejected it.[91]

Gettysburg became a postbellum focus of the "Lost Cause", a movement by writers such as Edward A. Pollard and Jubal Early to explain the reasons for

Figure 30: *Gettysburg, November 19, 1863. Crowd of citizens,
soldiers, and etc., with a red arrow indicating Abraham Lincoln*

the Confederate defeat in the war. A fundamental premise of their argument
was that the South was doomed because of the overwhelming advantage in
manpower and industrial might possessed by the North. They also contend
that Robert E. Lee, who up until this time had been almost invincible, was
betrayed by the failures of some of his key subordinates at Gettysburg: Ewell,
for failing to seize Cemetery Hill on July 1; Stuart, for depriving the army of
cavalry intelligence for a key part of the campaign; and especially Longstreet,
for failing to attack on July 2 as early and as forcefully as Lee had originally
intended. In this view, Gettysburg was seen as a great lost opportunity, in
which a decisive victory by Lee could have meant the end of the war in the
Confederacy's favor.[92]

After the war, General Pickett was asked why Confederates lost at Gettysburg.
He was reported to have said, "I always thought the Yankees had something to
do with it."

Gettysburg Address

The ravages of war were still evident in Gettysburg more than four months
later when, on November 19, the Soldiers' National Cemetery was dedicated.
During this ceremony, President Abraham Lincoln honored the fallen and re-
defined the purpose of the war in his historic Gettysburg Address.[93]

Figure 31: *Gettysburg National Cemetery*

Medal of Honor

There were 72 Medals of Honor awarded for the Gettysburg Campaign. 64 of
the awards were for actions taken during the battle itself, with the first recipient
being awarded in December 1864. The last Medal of Honor was posthumously
awarded to Lieutenant Alonzo Cushing in 2014.

Historical assessment

Decisive victory controversies

The nature of the result of the Battle of Gettysburg has been the subject of
controversy. Although not seen as overwhelmingly significant at the time,
particularly since the war continued for almost two years, in retrospect it has
often been cited as the "turning point", usually in combination with the fall of
Vicksburg the following day. This is based on the observation that, after Gettysburg, Lee's army conducted no more strategic offensives—his army merely
reacted to the initiative of Ulysses S. Grant in 1864 and 1865—and by the
speculative viewpoint of the Lost Cause writers that a Confederate victory at
Gettysburg might have resulted in the end of the war.[94]

<templatestyles src="Template:Quote_box/styles.css" />

[The Army of the Potomac] had won a victory. It might be less of a victory than
Mr. Lincoln had hoped for, but it was nevertheless a victory—and, because of

that, it was no longer possible for the Confederacy to win the war. The North might still lose it, to be sure, if the soldiers or the people should lose heart, but outright defeat was no longer in the cards.

Bruce Catton, *Glory Road*[95]

It is currently a widely held view that Gettysburg was a decisive victory for the Union, but the term is considered imprecise. It is inarguable that Lee's offensive on July 3 was turned back decisively and his campaign in Pennsylvania was terminated prematurely (although the Confederates at the time argued that this was a temporary setback and that the goals of the campaign were largely met). However, when the more common definition of "decisive victory" is intended—an indisputable military victory of a battle that determines or significantly influences the ultimate result of a conflict—historians are divided. For example, David J. Eicher called Gettysburg a "strategic loss for the Confederacy" and James M. McPherson wrote that "Lee and his men would go on to earn further laurels. But they never again possessed the power and reputation they carried into Pennsylvania those palmy summer days of 1863."[96]

However, Herman Hattaway and Archer Jones wrote that the "strategic impact of the Battle of Gettysburg was ... fairly limited." Steven E. Woodworth wrote that "Gettysburg proved only the near impossibility of decisive action in the Eastern theater." Edwin Coddington pointed out the heavy toll on the Army of the Potomac and that "after the battle Meade no longer possessed a truly effective instrument for the accomplishments of his task. The army needed a thorough reorganization with new commanders and fresh troops, but these changes were not made until Grant appeared on the scene in March 1864." Joseph T. Glatthaar wrote that "Lost opportunities and near successes plagued the Army of Northern Virginia during its Northern invasion," yet after Gettysburg, "without the distractions of duty as an invading force, without the breakdown of discipline, the Army of Northern Virginia [remained] an extremely formidable force." Ed Bearss wrote, "Lee's invasion of the North had been a costly failure. Nevertheless, at best the Army of the Potomac had simply preserved the strategic stalemate in the Eastern Theater ..."[97] Furthermore, the Confederacy soon proved it was still capable of winning significant victories over the Northern forces in both the East (Battle of Cold Harbor) and West (Battle of Chickamauga).

Peter Carmichael refers to the military context for the armies, the "horrendous losses at Chancellorsville and Gettysburg, which effectively destroyed Lee's offensive capacity," implying that these cumulative losses were not the result of a single battle. Thomas Goss, writing in the U.S. Army's *Military Review* journal on the definition of "decisive" and the application of that description to Gettysburg, concludes: "For all that was decided and accomplished, the Battle of Gettysburg fails to earn the label 'decisive battle'."[98] The military historian

Figure 32: *George G. Meade*

John Keegan agrees. Gettysburg was a landmark battle, the largest of the war and it would not be surpassed. The Union had restored to it the belief in certain victory, and the loss dispirited the Confederacy. If "not exactly a decisive battle", Gettysburg was the end of Confederate use of Northern Virginia as a military buffer zone, the setting for Grant's Overland Campaign.[99]

Lee vs. Meade

Prior to Gettysburg, Robert E. Lee had established a reputation as an almost invincible general, achieving stunning victories against superior numbers—although usually at the cost of high casualties to his army—during the Seven Days, the Northern Virginia Campaign (including the Second Battle of Bull Run), Fredericksburg, and Chancellorsville. Only the Maryland Campaign, with its tactically inconclusive Battle of Antietam, had been less than successful. Therefore, historians have attempted to explain how Lee's winning streak was interrupted so dramatically at Gettysburg. Although the issue is tainted by attempts to portray history and Lee's reputation in a manner supporting different partisan goals, the major factors in Lee's loss arguably can be attributed to: (1) his overconfidence in the invincibility of his men; (2) the performance of his subordinates, and his management thereof; (3) his failing health, and (4) the performance of his opponent, George G. Meade, and the Army of the Potomac.

Figure 33: *Robert E. Lee*

Throughout the campaign, Lee was influenced by the belief that his men were invincible; most of Lee's experiences with the Army of Northern Virginia had convinced him of this, including the great victory at Chancellorsville in early May and the rout of the Union troops at Gettysburg on July 1. Since morale plays an important role in military victory when other factors are equal, Lee did not want to dampen his army's desire to fight and resisted suggestions, principally by Longstreet, to withdraw from the recently captured Gettysburg to select a ground more favorable to his army. War correspondent Peter W. Alexander wrote that Lee "acted, probably, under the impression that his troops were able to carry any position however formidable. If such was the case, he committed an error, such however as the ablest commanders will sometimes fall into." Lee himself concurred with this judgment, writing to President Davis, "No blame can be attached to the army for its failure to accomplish what was projected by me, nor should it be censured for the unreasonable expectations of the public—I am alone to blame, in perhaps expecting too much of its prowess and valor."[100]

The most controversial assessments of the battle involve the performance of Lee's subordinates. The dominant theme of the Lost Cause writers and many other historians is that Lee's senior generals failed him in crucial ways, directly causing the loss of the battle; the alternative viewpoint is that Lee did not manage his subordinates adequately, and did not thereby compensate for their shortcomings.[101] Two of his corps commanders—Richard S. Ewell and A.P. Hill—had only recently been promoted and were not fully accustomed to Lee's style of command, in which he provided only general objectives and guidance to their former commander, Stonewall Jackson; Jackson translated these into detailed, specific orders to his division commanders.[102] All four of Lee's principal commanders received criticism during the campaign and battle:[103]

- James Longstreet suffered most severely from the wrath of the Lost Cause authors, not the least because he directly criticized Lee in postbellum writings and became a Republican after the war. His critics accuse him of attacking much later than Lee intended on July 2, squandering a chance to hit the Union Army before its defensive positions had firmed up. They also question his lack of motivation to attack strongly on July 2 and 3 because he had argued that the army should have maneuvered to a place where it would force Meade to attack them. The alternative view is that Lee was in close contact with Longstreet during the battle, agreed to delays on the morning of July 2, and never criticized Longstreet's performance. (There is also considerable speculation about what an attack might have looked like before Dan Sickles moved the III Corps toward the Peach Orchard.)[104]

- J.E.B. Stuart deprived Lee of cavalry intelligence during a good part of the campaign by taking his three best brigades on a path away from the army's. This arguably led to Lee's surprise at Hooker's vigorous pursuit; the engagement on July 1 that escalated into the full battle prematurely; and it also prevented Lee from understanding the full disposition of the enemy on July 2. The disagreements regarding Stuart's culpability for the situation originate in the relatively vague orders issued by Lee, but most modern historians agree that both generals were responsible to some extent for the failure of the cavalry's mission early in the campaign.[105]

- Richard S. Ewell has been universally criticized for failing to seize the high ground on the afternoon of July 1. Once again the disagreement centers on Lee's orders, which provided general guidance for Ewell to act "if practicable." Many historians speculate that Stonewall Jackson, if he had survived Chancellorsville, would have aggressively seized Culp's Hill, rendering Cemetery Hill indefensible, and changing the entire complexion of the battle. A differently worded order from Lee might have made the difference with this subordinate.[106]

- A.P. Hill has received some criticism for his ineffective performance. His actions caused the battle to begin and then escalate on July 1, despite Lee's orders not to bring on a general engagement (although historians point out that Hill kept Lee well informed of his actions during the day).

Figure 34: *Winfield S. Hancock*

However, Hill's illness minimized his personal involvement in the remainder of the battle, and Lee took the explicit step of temporarily removing troops from Hill's corps and giving them to Longstreet for Pickett's Charge.[107]

In addition to Hill's illness, Lee's performance was affected by heart troubles, which would eventually lead to his death in 1870; he had been diagnosed with pericarditis by his staff physicians in March 1863, though modern doctors believe he had in fact suffered a heart attack. He wrote to Jefferson Davis that his physical condition prevented him from offering full supervision in the field, and said, "I am so dull that in making use of the eyes of others I am frequently misled."[108]

As a final factor, Lee faced a new and formidable opponent in George G. Meade, and the Army of the Potomac fought well on its home territory. Although new to his army command, Meade deployed his forces relatively effectively; relied on strong subordinates such as Winfield S. Hancock to make decisions where and when they were needed; took great advantage of defensive positions; nimbly shifted defensive resources on interior lines to parry strong threats; and, unlike some of his predecessors, stood his ground throughout the battle in the face of fierce Confederate attacks.

Lee was quoted before the battle as saying Meade "would commit no blunders on my front and if I make one ... will make haste to take advantage of it." That prediction proved to be correct at Gettysburg. Stephen Sears wrote, "The fact of the matter is that George G. Meade, unexpectedly and against all odds, thoroughly outgeneraled Robert E. Lee at Gettysburg." Edwin B. Coddington wrote that the soldiers of the Army of the Potomac received a "sense of triumph which grew into an imperishable faith in [themselves]. The men knew what they could do under an extremely competent general; one of lesser ability and courage could well have lost the battle."[109]

Meade had his own detractors as well. Similar to the situation with Lee, Meade suffered partisan attacks about his performance at Gettysburg, but he had the misfortune of experiencing them in person. Supporters of his predecessor, Maj. Gen. Joseph Hooker, lambasted Meade before the U.S. Congress's Joint Committee on the Conduct of the War, where Radical Republicans suspected that Meade was a Copperhead and tried in vain to relieve him from command. Daniel E. Sickles and Daniel Butterfield accused Meade of planning to retreat from Gettysburg during the battle. Most politicians, including Lincoln, criticized Meade for what they considered to be his half-hearted pursuit of Lee after the battle. A number of Meade's most competent subordinates—Winfield S. Hancock, John Gibbon, Gouverneur K. Warren, and Henry J. Hunt, all heroes of the battle—defended Meade in print, but Meade was embittered by the overall experience.[110]

Battlefield preservation

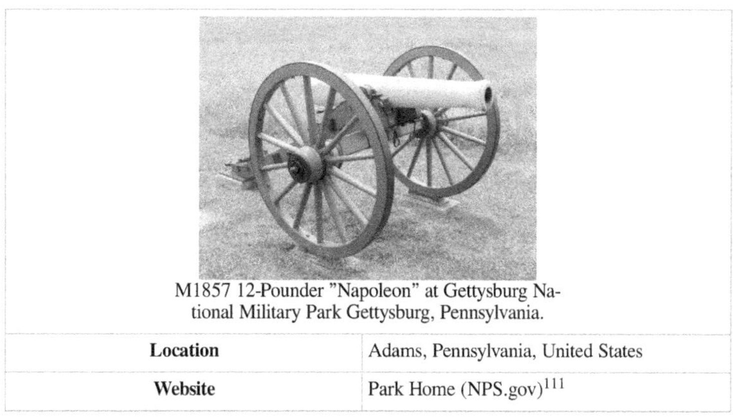

M1857 12-Pounder "Napoleon" at Gettysburg National Military Park Gettysburg, Pennsylvania.

Location	Adams, Pennsylvania, United States
Website	Park Home (NPS.gov)[111]

Today, the Gettysburg National Cemetery and Gettysburg National Military Park are maintained by the U.S. National Park Service as two of the nation's most revered historical landmarks. Although Gettysburg is one of the best known of all Civil War battlefields, it too faces threats to its preservation and interpretation. Many historically significant locations on the battlefield lie outside the boundaries of Gettysburg National Military Park and are vulnerable to residential or commercial development.

On July 20, 2009, a Comfort Inn and Suites opened on Cemetery Hill, adjacent to Evergreen Cemetery, just one of many modern edifices infringing on the historic field. The Baltimore Pike corridor attracts development that concerns preservationists.

Some preservation successes have emerged in recent years. Two proposals to open a casino at Gettysburg were defeated in 2006 and most recently in 2011, when public pressure forced the Pennsylvania Gaming Control Board to reject the proposed gambling hub at the intersection of Routes 15 and 30, near East Cavalry Field.[112] The Civil War Trust also successfully purchased and transferred 95 acres at the former site of the Gettysburg Country Club to the control of the U.S. Department of the Interior in 2011.

Less than half of the over 11,500 acres on the old Gettysburg Battlefield have been preserved for posterity thus far. The Civil War Trust (a division of the American Battlefield Trust) and its partners have acquired and preserved 1,022 acres (4.14 km^2) of the battlefield in more than 30 separate transactions since 1997.[113] Some of these acres are now among the 4,998 acres of the Gettysburg National Military Park. In 2015, the Trust made one of its most important and expensive acquisitions, paying $6 million for a four-acre parcel that included the stone house that Confederate Gen. Robert E. Lee used as his headquarters during the battle. The Trust razed a motel, restaurant and other buildings within the parcel to restore Lee's Headquarters and the site to their wartime appearance, adding interpretive signs. It opened the site to the public in October, 2016.[114]

Commemoration in U.S. postage and coinage

During the Civil War Centennial, the U.S. Post Office issued five postage stamps commemorating the 100th anniversaries of famous battles, as they occurred over a four-year period, beginning with the Battle of Fort Sumter Centennial issue of 1961. The Battle of Shiloh commemorative stamp was issued in 1962, the Battle of Gettysburg in 1963, the Battle of the Wilderness in 1964, and the Appomattox Centennial commemorative stamp in 1965. A commemorative half dollar for the battle was produced in 1936. As was typical for the period, mintage for the coin was very low, just 26,928. On January 24, 2011, the America the Beautiful quarters released a 25-cent coin commemorating Gettysburg National Military Park and the Battle of Gettysburg. The

Figure 35: *The 1936 Battle of Gettysburg half dollar*

Figure 36: *Gettysburg Centennial Commemorative issue of 1963*

Figure 37: *Gettysburg National Military Park Quarter, issued 2011*

reverse side of the coin depicts the monument on Cemetery Ridge to the 72nd Pennsylvania Infantry.

In popular culture

Film records survive of two Gettysburg reunions, held on the battlefield. At the 50th anniversary (1913), veterans re-enacted Pickett's Charge in a spirit of reconciliation, a meeting that carried great emotional force for both sides. At the 75th anniversary (1938), 2500 veterans attended, and there was a ceremonial mass hand-shake across a stone wall. This was recorded on sound film, and some Confederates can be heard giving the Rebel Yell.

The Battle of Gettysburg was depicted in the 1993 film *Gettysburg*, based on Michael Shaara's 1974 novel *The Killer Angels*. The film and novel focused primarily on the actions of Joshua Lawrence Chamberlain, John Buford, Robert E. Lee, and James Longstreet during the battle. The first day focused on Buford's cavalry defense, the second day on Chamberlain's defense at Little Round Top, and the third day on Pickett's Charge.

The south winning the Battle of Gettysburg is a popular premise for a point of divergence in American Civil War alternate histories. Here are some examples which either depict or make significant reference to an alternate Battle of Gettysburg (sometimes simply inserting fantasy or sci-fi elements in an account of the battle):

- Novels: *Bring the Jubilee* by Ward Moore; *If the South Had Won the Civil War* by Mackinlay Kantor; Civil War Trilogy (*Gettysburg, Grant Comes East, Never Call Retreat*) by Newt Gingrich, William R. Forstchen, and Albert S. Hanser; *Stonewall Jackson at Gettysburg* by Douglas Lee Gibboney; *By Force of Arms* by Billy Bennett. Also: Harry Turtledove's Southern Victory series has an analogous battle taking place at Camp Hill, another southeast Pennsylvania town.
- Short fiction: "If Lee Had NOT Won the Battle of Gettysburg" by Winston Churchill in *If It Had Happened Otherwise* and *If, or History Rewritten*, "Sidewise in Time" by Murray Leinster in various collections, "A Hard Day for Mother" by William R. Forstchen in *Alternate Generals* 1, "An Old Man's Summer" by Esther Friesner also in AG 1, "If the Lost Order Hadn't Been Lost" by James M. McPherson in *What If?* and *What Ifs? of American History*, "East of Appomattox" by Lee Allred in *Alternate Generals*

References

- Bearss, Edwin C. *Fields of Honor: Pivotal Battles of the Civil War*. Washington, D.C.: National Geographic Society, 2006. <templatestyles src="Module:Citation/CS1/styles.css" />ISBN 0-7922-7568-3.
- Busey, John W., and David G. Martin. *Regimental Strengths and Losses at Gettysburg*, 4th ed. Hightstown, NJ: Longstreet House, 2005. <templatestyles src="Module:Citation/CS1/styles.css" />ISBN 0-944413-67-6.
- Carmichael, Peter S., ed. *Audacity Personified: The Generalship of Robert E. Lee*. Baton Rouge: Louisiana State University Press, 2004. <templatestyles src="Module:Citation/CS1/styles.css" />ISBN 0-8071-2929-1.
- Catton, Bruce. *Glory Road*. Garden City, NY: Doubleday and Company, 1952. <templatestyles src="Module:Citation/CS1/styles.css" />ISBN 0-385-04167-5.
- Clark, Champ, and the Editors of Time-Life Books. *Gettysburg: The Confederate High Tide*. Alexandria, VA: Time-Life Books, 1985. <templatestyles src="Module:Citation/CS1/styles.css" />ISBN 0-8094-4758-4.
- Coddington, Edwin B. *The Gettysburg Campaign; a study in command*. New York: Scribner's, 1968. <templatestyles src="Module:Citation/CS1/styles.css" />ISBN 0-684-84569-5.

- Donald, David Herbert. *Lincoln*. New York: Simon & Schuster, 1995. <templatestyles src="Module:Citation/CS1/styles.css" />ISBN 0-684-80846-3.
- Eicher, David J. *The Longest Night: A Military History of the Civil War*. New York: Simon & Schuster, 2001. <templatestyles src="Module:Citation/CS1/styles.css" />ISBN 0-684-84944-5.
- Esposito, Vincent J. *West Point Atlas of American Wars*. New York: Frederick A. Praeger, 1959. <templatestyles src="Module:Citation/CS1/styles.css" />OCLC 5890637[115]. The collection of maps (without explanatory text) is available online at the West Point website[116].
- Foote, Shelby. *The Civil War: A Narrative*. Vol. 2, *Fredericksburg to Meridian*. New York: Random House, 1958. <templatestyles src="Module:Citation/CS1/styles.css" />ISBN 0-394-49517-9.
- Fuller, Maj. Gen. J. F. C. *Grant and Lee: A Study in Personality and Generalship*. Bloomington: Indiana University Press, 1957. <templatestyles src="Module:Citation/CS1/styles.css" />ISBN 0-253-13400-5.
- Gallagher, Gary W. *Lee and His Army in Confederate History*. Chapel Hill: University of North Carolina Press, 2001. <templatestyles src="Module:Citation/CS1/styles.css" />ISBN 978-0-8078-2631-7.
- Gallagher, Gary W. *Lee and His Generals in War and Memory*. Baton Rouge: Louisiana State University Press, 1998. <templatestyles src="Module:Citation/CS1/styles.css" />ISBN 0-8071-2958-5.
- Glatthaar, Joseph T. *General Lee's Army: From Victory to Collapse*. New York: Free Press, 2008. <templatestyles src="Module:Citation/CS1/styles.css" />ISBN 978-0-684-82787-2.
- Harman, Troy D. *Lee's Real Plan at Gettysburg*. Mechanicsburg, PA: Stackpole Books, 2003. <templatestyles src="Module:Citation/CS1/styles.css" />ISBN 0-8117-0054-2.
- Hattaway, Herman, and Archer Jones. *How the North Won: A Military History of the Civil War*. Urbana: University of Illinois Press, 1983. <templatestyles src="Module:Citation/CS1/styles.css" />ISBN 0-252-00918-5.
- Keegan, John. *The American Civil War: A Military History*. New York: Alfred A. Knopf, 2009. <templatestyles src="Module:Citation/CS1/styles.css" />ISBN 978-0-307-26343-8.
- Longacre, Edward G. *The Cavalry at Gettysburg*. Lincoln: University of Nebraska Press, 1986. <templatestyles src="Module:Citation/CS1/styles.css" />ISBN 0-8032-7941-8.
- McPherson, James M. *Battle Cry of Freedom: The Civil War Era*. Oxford History of the United States. New York: Oxford University Press, 1988. <templatestyles src="Module:Citation/CS1/styles.css" />ISBN 0-

19-503863-0.

- Martin, David G. *Gettysburg July 1*. rev. ed. Conshohocken, PA: Combined Publishing, 1996. <templatestyles src="Module:Citation/CS1/styles.css" />ISBN 0-938289-81-0.
- Murray, Williamson and Wayne Wei-siang Hsieh. "A Savage War:A Military History of the Civil War". Princeton: Princeton University Press, 2016. <templatestyles src="Module:Citation/CS1/styles.css" />ISBN 978-0-69-116940-8.
- Nye, Wilbur S. *Here Come the Rebels!* Dayton, OH: Morningside House, 1984. <templatestyles src="Module:Citation/CS1/styles.css" />ISBN 0-89029-080-6. First published in 1965 by Louisiana State University Press.
- Pfanz, Harry W. *Gettysburg – The First Day*. Chapel Hill: University of North Carolina Press, 2001. <templatestyles src="Module:Citation/CS1/styles.css" />ISBN 0-8078-2624-3.
- Pfanz, Harry W. *Gettysburg – The Second Day*. Chapel Hill: University of North Carolina Press, 1987. <templatestyles src="Module:Citation/CS1/styles.css" />ISBN 0-8078-1749-X.
- Pfanz, Harry W. *Gettysburg: Culp's Hill and Cemetery Hill*. Chapel Hill: University of North Carolina Press, 1993. <templatestyles src="Module:Citation/CS1/styles.css" />ISBN 0-8078-2118-7.
- Rawley, James A. (1966). *Turning Points of the Civil War*[117]. University of Nebraska Press. ISBN <bdi>0-8032-8935-9</bdi>. OCLC 44957745[118].<templatestyles src="Module:Citation/CS1/styles.css"></templatestyles>
- Sauers, Richard A. "Battle of Gettysburg." In *Encyclopedia of the American Civil War: A Political, Social, and Military History*, edited by David S. Heidler and Jeanne T. Heidler. New York: W. W. Norton & Company, 2000. <templatestyles src="Module:Citation/CS1/styles.css" />ISBN 0-393-04758-X.
- Sears, Stephen W. *Gettysburg*. Boston: Houghton Mifflin, 2003. <templatestyles src="Module:Citation/CS1/styles.css" />ISBN 0-395-86761-4.
- Symonds, Craig L. *American Heritage History of the Battle of Gettysburg*. New York: HarperCollins, 2001. <templatestyles src="Module:Citation/CS1/styles.css" />ISBN 0-06-019474-X.
- Tagg, Larry. *The Generals of Gettysburg*[119]. Campbell, CA: Savas Publishing, 1998. <templatestyles src="Module:Citation/CS1/styles.css" />ISBN 1-882810-30-9.
- Trudeau, Noah Andre. *Gettysburg: A Testing of Courage*. New York: HarperCollins, 2002. <templatestyles src="Module:Citation/CS1/styles.css" />ISBN 0-06-019363-8.
- Tucker, Glenn. *High Tide at Gettysburg*. Dayton, OH: Morningside

House, 1983. <templatestyles src="Module:Citation/CS1/styles.css" />ISBN 978-0-914427-82-7. First published 1958 by Bobbs-Merrill Co.

- Wert, Jeffry D. *Gettysburg: Day Three*. New York: Simon & Schuster, 2001. <templatestyles src="Module:Citation/CS1/styles.css" />ISBN 0-684-85914-9.
- White, Ronald C., Jr. *The Eloquent President: A Portrait of Lincoln Through His Words*. New York: Random House, 2005. <templatestyles src="Module:Citation/CS1/styles.css" />ISBN 1-4000-6119-9.
- Wittenberg, Eric J., J. David Petruzzi, and Michael F. Nugent. *One Continuous Fight: The Retreat from Gettysburg and the Pursuit of Lee's Army of Northern Virginia, July 4–14, 1863*. New York: Savas Beatie, 2008. <templatestyles src="Module:Citation/CS1/styles.css" />ISBN 978-1-932714-43-2.
- Woodworth, Steven E. *Beneath a Northern Sky: A Short History of the Gettysburg Campaign*. Wilmington, DE: SR Books (scholarly Resources, Inc.), 2003. <templatestyles src="Module:Citation/CS1/styles.css" />ISBN 0-8420-2933-8.

Memoirs and primary sources

- Paris, Louis-Philippe-Albert d'Orléans. *The Battle of Gettysburg: A History of the Civil War in America*[120]. Digital Scanning, Inc., 1999. <templatestyles src="Module:Citation/CS1/styles.css" />ISBN 1-58218-066-0. First published 1869 by Germer Baillière.
- New York (State), William F. Fox, and Daniel Edgar Sickles. *New York at Gettysburg: Final Report on the Battlefield of Gettysburg*[121]. Albany, NY: J.B. Lyon Company, Printers, 1900. <templatestyles src="Module:Citation/CS1/styles.css" />OCLC 607395975[122].
- U.S. War Department, *The War of the Rebellion*[123]: *a Compilation of the Official Records of the Union and Confederate Armies*. Washington, DC: U.S. Government Printing Office, 1880–1901.

Further reading

External media

Images
🔍 GettysburgPhotographs.com[124]
🔍 Battlefields.org maps & photos[125]
🔍 Gettysburg.edu paintings & photos[126]
Video

📖 GettysburgAnimated.com[127]

- Adkin, Mark. *The Gettysburg Companion: The Complete Guide to America's Most Famous Battle*. Mechanicsburg, PA: Stackpole Books, 2008. <templatestyles src="Module:Citation/CS1/styles.css" />ISBN 978-0-8117-0439-7.
- Bachelder, John B. *The Bachelder Papers: Gettysburg in Their Own Words*. Edited by David L. Ladd and Audrey J. Ladd. 3 vols. Dayton, OH: Morningside Press, 1994. <templatestyles src="Module:Citation/CS1/styles.css" />ISBN 0-89029-320-1.
- Bachelder, John B. *Gettysburg: What to See, and How to See It: Embodying Full Information for Visiting the Field*[128]. Boston: Bachelder, 1873. <templatestyles src="Module:Citation/CS1/styles.css" />OCLC 4637523[129].
- Ballard, Ted, and Billy Arthur. *Gettysburg Staff Ride Briefing Book*[130]. Carlisle, PA: United States Army Center of Military History, 1999. <templatestyles src="Module:Citation/CS1/styles.css" />OCLC 42908450[131].
- Bearss, Edwin C. *Receding Tide: Vicksburg and Gettysburg: The Campaigns That Changed the Civil War*. Washington, D.C.: National Geographic Society, 2010. <templatestyles src="Module:Citation/CS1/styles.css" />ISBN 978-1-4262-0510-1.
- Boritt, Gabor S., ed. *The Gettysburg Nobody Knows*. New York: Oxford University Press, 1997. <templatestyles src="Module:Citation/CS1/styles.css" />ISBN 0-19-510223-1.
- Desjardin, Thomas A. *These Honored Dead: How the Story of Gettysburg Shaped American Memory*. New York: Da Capo Press, 2003. <templatestyles src="Module:Citation/CS1/styles.css" />ISBN 0-306-81267-3.
- Frassanito, William A. *Early Photography at Gettysburg*. Gettysburg, PA: Thomas Publications, 1995. <templatestyles src="Module:Citation/CS1/styles.css" />ISBN 1-57747-032-X.
- Lyon Fremantle, Arthur J. *The Fremantle Diary: A Journal of the Confederacy*. Edited by Walter Lord. Short Hills, NJ: Burford Books, 2002. <templatestyles src="Module:Citation/CS1/styles.css" />ISBN 1-58080-085-8. First published 1954 by Capicorn Books.
- Gallagher, Gary W., ed. *Three Days at Gettysburg: Essays on Confederate and Union Leadership*. Kent, OH: Kent State University Press, 1999. <templatestyles src="Module:Citation/CS1/styles.css" />ISBN 0-87338-629-9.
- Gottfried, Bradley M. *Brigades of Gettysburg*. New York: Da Capo Press, 2002. <templatestyles src="Module:Citation/CS1/styles.css" />ISBN 0-306-81175-8.

- Gottfried, Bradley M. *The Maps of Gettysburg: An Atlas of the Gettysburg Campaign, June 3–13, 1863*. New York: Savas Beatie, 2007. <templatestyles src="Module:Citation/CS1/styles.css" />ISBN 978-1-932714-30-2.
- Grimsley, Mark, and Brooks D. Simpson. *Gettysburg: A Battlefield Guide*. Lincoln: University of Nebraska Press, 1999. <templatestyles src="Module:Citation/CS1/styles.css" />ISBN 0-8032-7077-1.
- Guelzo, Allen C. *Gettysburg: The Last Invasion*. New York: Vintage Books, 2013. <templatestyles src="Module:Citation/CS1/styles.css" />ISBN 978-0-307-74069-4. First published in 2013 by Alfred A. Knopf.
- Hall, Jeffrey C. *The Stand of the U.S. Army at Gettysburg*. Bloomington: Indiana University Press, 2003. <templatestyles src="Module:Citation/CS1/styles.css" />ISBN 0-253-34258-9.
- Haskell, Frank Aretas. *The Battle of Gettysburg*. Whitefish, MT: Kessinger Publishing, 2006. <templatestyles src="Module:Citation/CS1/styles.css" />ISBN 978-1-4286-6012-0.
- Hawthorne, Frederick W. *Gettysburg: Stories of Men and Monuments*. Gettysburg, PA: Association of Licensed Battlefield Guides, 1988. <templatestyles src="Module:Citation/CS1/styles.css" />ISBN 0-9657444-0-X.
- Hoptak, John David. *Confrontation at Gettysburg: A Nation Saved, a Cause Lost*. Charleston, SC: The History Press, 2012. <templatestyles src="Module:Citation/CS1/styles.css" />ISBN 978-1-60949-426-1.
- Huntington, Tom. *Pennsylvania Civil War Trails: The Guide to Battle Sites, Monuments, Museums and Towns*. Mechanicsburg, PA: Stackpole Books, 2007. <templatestyles src="Module:Citation/CS1/styles.css" />ISBN 978-0-8117-3379-3.
- Laino, Philip, *Gettysburg Campaign Atlas*, 2nd ed. Dayton, OH: Gatehouse Press 2009. <templatestyles src="Module:Citation/CS1/styles.css" />ISBN 978-1-934900-45-1.
- McMurry, Richard M. "The Pennsylvania Gambit and the Gettysburg Splash". In *The Gettysburg Nobody Knows*, edited by Gabor Boritt. New York: Oxford University Press, 1997. <templatestyles src="Module:Citation/CS1/styles.css" />ISBN 0-19-510223-1.
- McPherson, James M. *Hallowed Ground: A Walk at Gettysburg*. New York: Crown Publishers, 2003. <templatestyles src="Module:Citation/CS1/styles.css" />ISBN 0-609-61023-6.
- Petruzzi, J. David, and Steven Stanley. *The Complete Gettysburg Guide*. New York: Savas Beatie, 2009. <templatestyles src="Module:Citation/CS1/styles.css" />ISBN 978-1-932714-63-0.
- Shaara, Michael. *The Killer Angels: A Novel*. New York: Ballantine Books, 2001. <templatestyles src="Module:Citation/CS1/styles.css" />ISBN 978-0-345-44412-7. First published 1974 by David McKay Co.

- Stackpole, Gen. Edward J. *They Met at Gettysburg*. Harrisburg, PA: Stackpole Books, 1956, <templatestyles src="Module:Citation/CS1/styles.css" />OCLC 22643644[132].

External links

 Wikimedia Commons has media related to <wbr />*Battle of Gettysburg*, <wbr />*Gettysburg Battlefield* and <wbr />*Gettysburg National Military Park*.

- Battle of Gettysburg[125]: **Battle Maps**[133], histories, photos, and preservation news (American Battlefield Trust)
- **Animated map** of the Battle of Gettysburg[134] (American Battlefield Trust)
- Gettysburg National Military Park (National Park Service)[135]
- Papers of the Gettysburg National Military Park seminars[136]
- U.S. Army's Interactive Battle of Gettysburg with Narratives[137]
- Military History Online: The Battle of Gettysburg[138]
- Official Records: The Battle of Gettysburg[139]
- The Brothers War: The Battle of Gettysburg[140]
- Gettysburg Discussion Group archives[141]
- List of 53 Confederate generals at Gettysburg[142]
- Encyclopædia Britannica: Battle of Gettysburg[143]
- National Park Service battle description[144]
- A film clip "Blue and Gray At 75th Anniversary of Great Battle, 1938/07/04 (1938)"[145] is available at the Internet Archive

<indicator name="good-star"> ⊕ </indicator>

Killed: Day 1 -July 1st, 1863

John F. Reynolds

John Reynolds	
Born	September 21, 1820 Lancaster, Pennsylvania
Died	July 1, 1863 (aged 42) Gettysburg, Pennsylvania
Place of burial	Lancaster Cemetery, Lancaster, Pennsylvania
Allegiance	United States of America Union
Service/<wbr/>branch	United States Army Union Army
Years of service	1841–1863
Rank	Major General
Commands held	I Corps, Army of the Potomac

Battles/-wars	Mexican–American War • Battle of Monterrey • Battle of Buena Vista American Civil War • Seven Days Battles • Second Battle of Bull Run • Battle of Fredericksburg • Battle of Chancellorsville • Battle of Gettysburg †

John Fulton Reynolds (September 21, 1820 – July 1, 1863)[146] was a career United States Army officer and a general in the American Civil War. One of the Union Army's most respected senior commanders, he played a key role in committing the Army of the Potomac to the Battle of Gettysburg and was killed at the start of the battle.

Early life and career

Reynolds was born in Lancaster, Pennsylvania, one of nine surviving children of John Reynolds (1787–1853) and Lydia Moore Reynolds (1794–1843). Two of his brothers were James LeFevre Reynolds, Quartermaster General of Pennsylvania, and Rear Admiral Will Reynolds.[147] Prior to his military training, Reynolds studied in nearby Lititz, about 6 miles (9.7 km) from his home in Lancaster. Next he attended a school in Long Green, Maryland, and finally the Lancaster County Academy.[148]

Reynolds was nominated to the United States Military Academy in 1837 by Senator James Buchanan, a family friend, and graduated 26th of 50 cadets in the class of 1841. He was commissioned a brevet second lieutenant in the 3rd U.S. Artillery, assigned to Fort McHenry. From 1842 to 1845 he was assigned to St. Augustine, Florida, and Fort Moultrie, South Carolina, before joining Zachary Taylor's army at Corpus Christi, Texas, for the Mexican–American War. He was awarded two brevet promotions in Mexico—to captain for gallantry at Monterrey and to major for Buena Vista, where his section of guns prevented the Mexican cavalry from outflanking the American left.[149] During the war, he became friends with fellow officers Winfield Scott Hancock and Lewis A. Armistead.

On his return from Mexico, Reynolds was assigned to Fort Preble, Maine, New Orleans, Louisiana, and Fort Lafayette, New York. He was next sent west to Fort Orford, Oregon, in 1855, and participated in the Rogue River Wars of 1856 and the Utah War with the Mormons in 1857-58. He was the Commandant of Cadets at West Point from September 1860 to June 1861, while also serving as an instructor of artillery, cavalry, and infantry tactics. During his return from the West, Reynolds became engaged to Katherine May Hewitt. Since they were from different religious denominations—Reynolds was a Protestant, Hewitt a Catholic—the engagement was kept a secret and Hewitt's parents did not learn about it until after Reynolds' death.[150]

Civil War

Early assignments and the Seven Days

Soon after the start of the Civil War, Reynolds was offered the position as aide-de-camp to Lt. Gen. Winfield Scott, but declined. He was appointed lieutenant colonel of the 14th U.S. Infantry, but before he could engage with that unit, he was promoted to brigadier general on August 20, 1861, and ordered to report to Washington, D.C. While in transit, his orders were changed to report to Cape Hatteras Inlet, North Carolina. Maj. Gen. George B. McClellan intervened with the Secretary of War to get his orders changed once again, assigning him to the newly formed Army of the Potomac. His first assignment was with a board that examined the qualifications of volunteer officers, but he soon was given command of a brigade of Pennsylvania Reserves.[151]

As McClellan's army moved up the Virginia Peninsula in the 1862 Peninsula Campaign, Reynolds occupied and became military governor of Fredericksburg, Virginia. His brigade was then ordered to join the V Corps at Mechanicsville, just before the start of the Seven Days Battles. The brigade was hit hard by the Confederate attack of June 26 at the Battle of Beaver Dam Creek, but their defensive line held and Reynolds later received a letter of commendation from his division commander, Brig. Gen. George A. McCall.[152]

The Confederate attack continued on June 27 and Reynolds, exhausted from the Battle of Gaines' Mill and two days without sleep, was captured in Boatswain's Swamp, Virginia. Thinking he was in a place of relative safety, he fell asleep and was not aware that his retreating troops left him behind. He was extremely embarrassed when brought before the Confederate general of the capturing troops; D.H. Hill was an Army friend and colleague from before the war. Hill allegedly told him, "Reynolds, do not feel so bad about your capture, it is the fate of wars."[153] Reynolds was transported to Richmond and held at Libby Prison, but was quickly exchanged on August 15 (for Lloyd Tilghman).[154]

Second Bull Run, Fredericksburg, and Chancellorsville

Upon his return, Reynolds was given command of the Pennsylvania Reserves Division, whose commander, McCall, had been captured just two days after Reynolds. The V Corps joined the Army of Virginia, under Maj. Gen. John Pope, at Manassas. On the second day of the Second Battle of Bull Run, while most of the Union Army was retreating, Reynolds led his men in a last-ditch

stand on Henry House Hill, site of the great Union debacle at First Bull Run
the previous year. Waving the flag of the 2nd Reserves regiment, he yelled,
"Now boys, give them the steel, charge bayonets, double quick!" His counterattack halted the Confederate advance long enough to give the Union Army
time to retreat in a more orderly fashion, arguably the most important factor
in preventing its complete destruction.[155]

At the request of Pennsylvania Governor Andrew G. Curtin, Reynolds was
given command of the Pennsylvania Militia during General Robert E. Lee's
invasion of Maryland. Generals McClellan and Joseph Hooker complained
that "a scared governor ought not to be permitted to destroy the usefulness of
an entire division," but the governor prevailed and Reynolds spent two weeks
in Pennsylvania drilling old men and boys, missing the Battle of Antietam.
However, he returned to the Army of the Potomac in late 1862 and assumed
command of the I Corps. One of his divisions, commanded by Maj. Gen.
George G. Meade, made the only breakthrough at the Battle of Fredericksburg,
but Reynolds did not reinforce Meade with his other two divisions and the
attack failed; Reynolds did not receive a clear understanding from Maj. Gen.
William B. Franklin about his role in the attack. After the battle, Reynolds was
promoted to major general of volunteers, with a date of rank of November 29,
1862.[156]

At the Battle of Chancellorsville in May 1863, Reynolds clashed with Maj.
Gen. Hooker, his predecessor at I Corps, but by this time the commander of

the Army of the Potomac. Hooker originally placed the I Corps on the extreme left of the Union line, southeast of Fredericksburg, hoping to threaten and distract the Confederate right. On May 2, Hooker changed his mind and ordered the corps to conduct a daylight march nearly 20 miles to swing around and become the extreme right flank of the army, to the northwest of the XI Corps. The march was delayed by faulty communications and by the need to move stealthily to avoid Confederate contact. Thus, the I Corps was not yet in position when the XI Corps was surprised and overrun by Lt. Gen. Thomas J. "Stonewall" Jackson's flank attack, a setback that destroyed Hooker's nerve for offensive action. Hooker called a council of war on May 4 in which Reynolds voted to proceed with the battle, but although the vote was three to two for offensive action, Hooker decided to retreat. Reynolds, who had gone to sleep after giving his proxy vote to Meade, woke up and muttered loud enough for Hooker to hear, "What was the use of calling us together at this time of night when he intended to retreat anyhow?" The 17,000-man I Corps was not engaged at Chancellorsville and suffered only 300 casualties during the entire campaign.[157]

Reynolds joined several of his fellow officers in urging that Hooker be replaced, in the same way he had spoken out against Maj. Gen. Ambrose Burnside after Fredericksburg. On the previous occasion, Reynolds wrote in a private letter, "If we do not get some one soon who can command an army without consulting 'Stanton and Halleck' at Washington, I do not know what will become of this Army." President Abraham Lincoln met with Reynolds in a private interview on June 2 and is believed to have asked him whether he would consider being the next commander of the Army of the Potomac. Reynolds supposedly replied that he would be willing to accept only if he were given a free hand and could be isolated from the political influences that had affected the Army commanders throughout the war. Unable to comply with his demands, Lincoln promoted the more junior George G. Meade to replace Hooker on June 28.[158]

Gettysburg

On the morning of July 1, 1863, Reynolds was commanding the "left wing" of the Army of the Potomac, with operational control over the I, III, and XI Corps, and Brig. Gen. John Buford's cavalry division. Buford occupied the town of Gettysburg, Pennsylvania, and set up light defensive lines north and west of the town. He resisted the approach of two Confederate infantry brigades on the Chambersburg Pike until the nearest Union infantry, Reynolds' I Corps, began to arrive. Reynolds rode out ahead of the 1st Division, met with Buford, and then accompanied some of his soldiers, probably from Brig. Gen. Lysander Cutler's brigade, into the fighting at Herbst's Woods. Troops began arriving from Brig. Gen. Solomon Meredith's Iron Brigade, and as Reynolds

Figure 38: *"The Fall of Reynolds" – drawing of Reynolds' death at Gettysburg*

was supervising the placement of the 2nd Wisconsin, he yelled at them, "Forward men forward for God's sake and drive those fellows out of those woods." At that moment he fell from his horse with a wound in the back of the upper neck, or lower head,[159] and died almost instantly. Command passed to his senior division commander, Maj. Gen. Abner Doubleday.

<templatestyles src="Template:Quote_box/styles.css" />

For the Union side, the death of John Reynolds meant more than the loss of an inspiring leader; it also removed from the equation the one person with enough vision and sense of purpose to manage this battle.

Noah Andre Trudeau, *Gettysburg: A Testing of Courage*[160]

The loss of General Reynolds was keenly felt by the army. He was loved by his men and respected by his peers. There are no recorded instances of negative comments made by his contemporaries.[161] Historian Shelby Foote wrote that many considered him "not only the highest ranking but also the best general in the army."[162] His death had a more immediate effect that day, however. By ratifying Buford's defensive plan and engaging his I Corps infantry, Reynolds essentially selected the location for the Battle of Gettysburg for Meade, turning a chance meeting engagement into a massive pitched battle, committing the Army of the Potomac to fight on that ground with forces that were initially numerically inferior to the Confederates that were concentrating there. In the command confusion that followed Reynolds' death, the two Union corps that reached the field were overwhelmed and forced to retreat through the streets

Figure 39: *Possible location of General Reynolds' death*

of Gettysburg to the high ground south of town, where they were rallied by his old friend, Maj. Gen. Winfield S. Hancock.[163]

Reynolds' body was immediately transported from Gettysburg to Taneytown, Maryland, and then to his birthplace, Lancaster, Pennsylvania, where he was buried on July 4, 1863. Befitting his importance to the Union and his native state, he is memorialized by three statues in Gettysburg National Military Park (an equestrian statue on McPherson Ridge, one by John Quincy Adams Ward in the National Cemetery, and one on the Pennsylvania Memorial),[164] as well as one in front of the Philadelphia City Hall.

Kate Hewitt had agreed with Reynolds that if he were killed in the war and they could not marry, she would join a convent. After he was buried, she traveled to Emmitsburg, Maryland, and joined the St. Joseph Central House of the Order of the Daughters of Charity.[165]

Death controversies

Historians disagree on the details of Reynolds' death, including the specific time (either 10:15 a.m. or 10:40–10:50 a.m.), the exact location (on East McPherson Ridge, near the 2nd Wisconsin Infantry, or West McPherson Ridge, near the 19th Indiana), and the source of the bullet (a Confederate infantryman, a Confederate sharpshooter, or friendly fire). One primary source

Figure 40: *"Where Reynolds Fell," (from*
The Photographic History of the Civil War)

was Sergeant Charles Henry Veil, his orderly and unit Color Guard, who described the events in a letter in 1864 and then contradicted some of the details
in another letter 45 years later. A letter from Reynolds' sister, Jennie, stated
that the wound had a downward trajectory from the neck, implying that he
was shot from above, presumably a sharpshooter in a tree or barn. Historians
Bruce Catton and Glenn Tucker make firm assertions that a sharpshooter was
responsible; Stephen Sears credits volley fire from the 7th Tennessee against
the 2nd Wisconsin; Edwin Coddington cites the sister's letter and finds the
sharpshooter theory to be partly credible, but leans towards Sears' conclusion;
Harry W. Pfanz agrees that the location was behind the 2nd Wisconsin, but
makes no judgment about the source of the fire. Steve Sanders, writing in
Gettysburg magazine, suggested the possibility of friendly fire based on some
accounts, and concludes that it is as equally likely as enemy fire.[166]

In popular media

Reynolds plays a role in Michael Shaara's 1974 Pulitzer Prize winning novel
The Killer Angels, as well as the 1993 film based on that novel, *Gettysburg* (in
which he was played by John Rothman). The film portrays Reynolds as being
deliberately targeted by a Confederate sharpshooter, a scene based on the Don

Troiani painting of the event. Reynolds is also significant in the prequel to *The Killer Angels*, Jeffrey Shaara's novel *Gods and Generals*, although his role was deleted from the 2003 film based on the novel.

A significant portion of the song "The Devil to Pay" by Jon Schaffer of Iced Earth in the Gettysburg trilogy is dedicated to John Reynolds, with the song "When Johnny Comes Marching Home" played and stylized using both electric guitar and an orchestra.

Monuments and memorials

Equestrian statue on McPherson Ridge, Chambersburg Pike, Gettysburg National Military Park, general view and closeup

Statue by John Quincy Adams Ward in the National Cemetery, Gettysburg National Military Park

In front of Philadelphia City Hall

Gettysburg, Penna

References

- Bearss, Edwin C. *Fields of Honor: Pivotal Battles of the Civil War*. Washington, DC: National Geographic Society, 2006. <templatestyles src="Module:Citation/CS1/styles.css" />ISBN 0-7922-7568-3.
- Carney, Stephen A. "John Fulton Reynolds." In *Encyclopedia of the American Civil War: A Political, Social, and Military History*, edited by David S. Heidler and Jeanne T. Heidler. New York: W. W. Norton & Company, 2000. <templatestyles src="Module:Citation/CS1/styles.css" />ISBN 0-393-04758-X.
- Coddington, Edwin B. *The Gettysburg Campaign; a study in command*. New York: Scribner's, 1968. <templatestyles src="Module:Citation/CS1/styles.css" />ISBN 0-684-84569-5.
- Eicher, John H., and David J. Eicher. *Civil War High Commands*. Stanford, CA: Stanford University Press, 2001. <templatestyles src="Module:Citation/CS1/styles.css" />ISBN 0-8047-3641-3.
- Foote, Shelby. *The Civil War: A Narrative*. Vol. 2, *Fredericksburg to Meridian*. New York: Random House, 1958. <templatestyles src="Module:Citation/CS1/styles.css" />ISBN 0-394-49517-9.

- Hawthorne, Frederick W. *Gettysburg: Stories of Men and Monuments*. Gettysburg, PA: Association of Licensed Battlefield Guides, 1988. <templatestyles src="Module:Citation/CS1/styles.css" />ISBN 0-9657444-0-X.
- Kantor, MacKinlay (1952), *Gettysburg*, New York: Random House. ["Friendly fire" theory.]
- Pfanz, Harry W. *Gettysburg – The First Day*. Chapel Hill: University of North Carolina Press, 2001. <templatestyles src="Module:Citation/CS1/styles.css" />ISBN 0-8078-2624-3.
- Sander, Steve. "Enduring Tales of Gettysburg: The Death of Reynolds". *The Gettysburg Magazine*. Issue 14, January 1996.
- Sears, Stephen W. *Gettysburg*. Boston: Houghton Mifflin, 2003. <templatestyles src="Module:Citation/CS1/styles.css" />ISBN 0-395-86761-4.
- Sears, Stephen W. *To the Gates of Richmond: The Peninsula Campaign*. Ticknor and Fields, 1992. <templatestyles src="Module:Citation/CS1/styles.css" />ISBN 0-89919-790-6.
- Tagg, Larry. *The Generals of Gettysburg*[167]. Campbell, CA: Savas Publishing, 1998. <templatestyles src="Module:Citation/CS1/styles.css" />ISBN 1-882810-30-9.
- Trudeau, Noah Andre. *Gettysburg: A Testing of Courage*. New York: HarperCollins, 2002. <templatestyles src="Module:Citation/CS1/styles.css" />ISBN 0-06-019363-8.
- Tucker, Glenn. *High Tide at Gettysburg*. Dayton, OH: Morningside House, 1983. <templatestyles src="Module:Citation/CS1/styles.css" />ISBN 978-0-914427-82-7. First published 1958 by Bobbs-Merrill Co.
- Warner, Ezra J. *Generals in Blue: Lives of the Union Commanders*. Baton Rouge: Louisiana State University Press, 1964. <templatestyles src="Module:Citation/CS1/styles.css" />ISBN 0-8071-0822-7.
- Welcher, Frank J. *The Union Army, 1861–1865 Organization and Operations*. Vol. 1, *The Eastern Theater*. Bloomington: Indiana University Press, 1989. <templatestyles src="Module:Citation/CS1/styles.css" />ISBN 0-253-36453-1.
- Reynolds family genealogy[168]

External links

 Wikimedia Commons has media related to *John Fulton Reynolds*.

- Works by or about John F. Reynolds[169] at Internet Archive
- "John F. Reynolds"[170]. Find a Grave. Retrieved 2008-02-12.<templatestyles src="Module:Citation/CS1/styles.css"></templatestyles>
- Reynolds family papers[171]
- Military biography of Reynolds[172] from the Cullum biographies
- Grand Army of the Republic in Lancaster County, Pennsylvania[173]

Military offices		
Preceded by **George G. Meade**	**Commander of the I Corps** **(Army of the Potomac)** September 29, 1862 – January 2, 1863	Succeeded by **James S. Wadsworth**
Preceded by **James S. Wadsworth**	**Commander of the I Corps** **(Army of the Potomac)** January 4, 1863 – March 1, 1863	Succeeded by **James S. Wadsworth**
Preceded by **James S. Wadsworth**	**Commander of the I Corps** **(Army of the Potomac)** March 9, 1863 – July 1, 1863	Succeeded by **Abner Doubleday**

Killed: Day 2 - July 2nd, 1863

William Barksdale

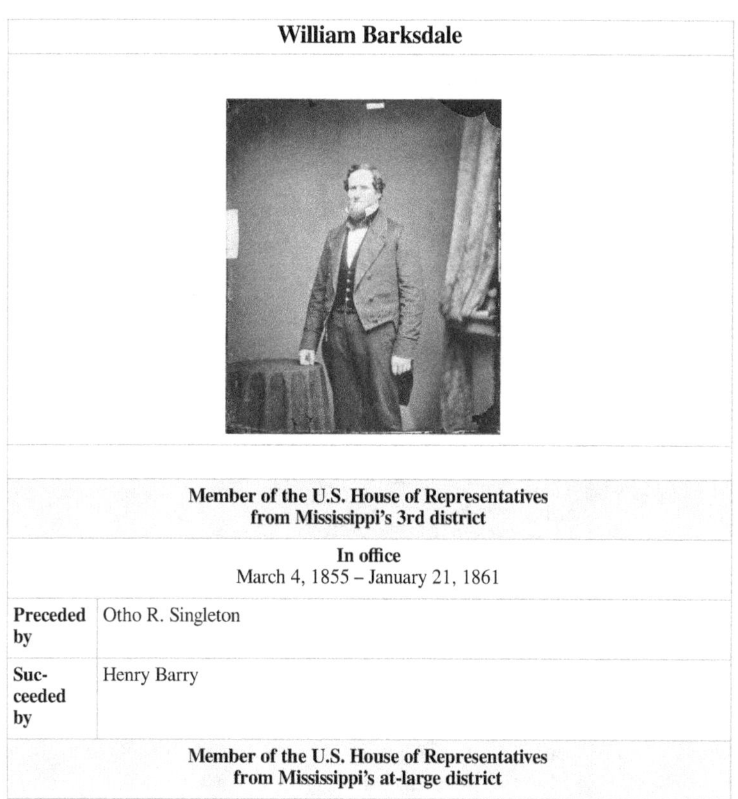

William Barksdale	
Member of the U.S. House of Representatives from Mississippi's 3rd district	
In office March 4, 1855 – January 21, 1861	
Preceded by	Otho R. Singleton
Succeeded by	Henry Barry
Member of the U.S. House of Representatives from Mississippi's at-large district	

In office March 4, 1853 – March 3, 1855	
Preceded by	*no at-large seats*
Succeeded by	*3rd Congressional District established*
Personal details	
Born	August 21, 1821 Smyrna, Tennessee
Died	July 3, 1863 (aged 41) Gettysburg, Pennsylvania
Resting place	Greenwood Cemetery Jackson, Mississippi
Political party	Democratic
Profession	Newspaper editor, soldier
Military service	
Allegiance	United States of America Confederate States of America
Branch/service	United States Army Confederate States Army
Years of service	1847–1848 (USA) 1861–1863 (CSA)
Rank	Captain (USA) Brigadier General (CSA)
Unit	2nd Mississippi Infantry (USA)
Commands	13th Mississippi Infantry (CSA) Barksdale's Mississippi Brigade
Battles/wars	Mexican–American War American Civil War • First Battle of Bull Run • Battle of Ball's Bluff • Peninsula Campaign • Seven Days Battles • Battle of Antietam • Battle of Fredericksburg • Battle of Chancellorsville • Battle of Gettysburg †

William Barksdale (August 21, 1821 – July 3, 1863) was a lawyer, newspaper editor, U.S. Congressman, slaveholder and a Confederate general in the American Civil War. A staunch secessionist, he was mortally wounded during the Battle of Gettysburg while leading his brigade's attack on Union forces not far from Cemetery Ridge.

Early life

William Barksdale was born in Smyrna, Tennessee, the son of William Barksdale and Nancy Hervey Lester Barksdale. He was the older brother of Ethelbert Barksdale, who would serve in both the antebellum U.S. Congress and then the Confederate States Congress during the Civil War. He was of English ancestry which came to America during the 1600s.[174]

Barksdale graduated from the University of Nashville and practiced law in Mississippi from the age of 21, but gave up his practice to become the editor of the *Columbus [Mississippi] Democrat*, a pro-slavery newspaper. He enlisted in the 2nd Mississippi Infantry Regiment and served in the Mexican War as a captain and quartermaster, but often participated in the infantry fighting as well.

After the war, he entered the U.S. House of Representatives and achieved national prominence as a States' rights Democrat, serving from March 4, 1853, to January 12, 1861. He was considered to be one of the most ferocious of all the "Fire-Eaters" in the House. He allegedly stood by the side of Representative Preston S. Brooks as Brooks attacked Massachusetts abolitionist Senator Charles Sumner in the Senate chamber with a cane, although he was not one of the members that the House tried to censure after the incident.

Before the start of the Civil War, Barksdale inadvertently helped stop one of the most notorious incidents of violence in U.S. legislative history. On February 5, 1858, a brawl between pro and anti-slavery legislators started on the House floor. During the melee, a missed punch from a fellow Congressman knocked his wig off, and an embarrassed Barksdale put it back on backwards, causing both sides to break out laughing and stopping the fight.

Civil War

After the state of Mississippi seceded just before the start of the Civil War, Barksdale resigned from Congress to become adjutant general, and then quartermaster general, of the Mississippi Militia, at the rank of brigadier general, with date of rank March 1, 1861. On May 1, he was appointed colonel in the Confederate States Army of the 13th Mississippi Infantry, a regiment that he led in the First Battle of Bull Run that summer, and the Battle of Ball's Bluff in October. The following spring, he took his regiment to the Virginia Peninsula and fought in the Peninsula Campaign and the Seven Days Battles. When his brigade commander, Brig. Gen. Richard Griffith, was mortally wounded at the Battle of Savage's Station on June 29, 1862, Barksdale assumed command

Figure 41: *General Barksdale's cenotaph in Greenwood Cemetery, Jackson, Mississippi.*

of the brigade and led it in an heroic, but bloody and futile, charge at the Battle of Malvern Hill. The brigade became known as "Barksdale's Mississippi Brigade." He was promoted to brigadier general on August 12, 1862.

In the Northern Virginia Campaign, Barksdale's Brigade was stationed at Harpers Ferry, and thus did not participate in the Second Battle of Bull Run. In the Maryland Campaign, his brigade was assigned to the division of Maj. Gen. Lafayette McLaws in Lt. Gen. James Longstreet's First Corps of the Army of Northern Virginia. It was one of the brigades that attacked Maryland Heights, leading to the surrender of the Union garrison at Harpers Ferry. At the subsequent Battle of Antietam, McLaws's Division defended the West Woods against the assault by Maj. Gen. John Sedgwick's division, saving the Confederate left flank. At the Battle of Fredericksburg, Barksdale's Brigade defended the waterfront of the city from Union forces attempting to cross the Rappahannock River, sniping at infantry and engineer forces from buildings that had been turned into rubble by Union artillery.[175]

At the Battle of Chancellorsville in May 1863, Barksdale's Brigade was one of the few units in James Longstreet's Corps that was present at the battle; most of the corps was detached for duty in Suffolk, Virginia. Once again, Barksdale's brigade defended the heights above Fredericksburg, this time against his previous adversary, Sedgwick, whose VI Corps was over ten times the size of his brigade. Sedgwick's assault was successful and Barksdale pulled back after delaying the Union force, but he was able to rally his brigade and retake the lost ground the next day.

At the Battle of Gettysburg, Barksdale's Brigade arrived with McLaws's Division after the first day of battle, July 1, 1863. The plan from General Robert E. Lee was for Longstreet's Corps to maneuver into position and attack northeast, up the Emmitsburg Road, to roll up the Union left flank. Barksdale's sector of the attack placed him directly at the tip of the salient in the Union line anchored at the Peach Orchard, defended by the Union III Corps. At about 5:30 p.m., Barksdale's Brigade burst from the woods and started an irresistible assault, which has been described as one of the most breathtaking spectacles of the Civil War. A Union colonel was quoted as saying, "It was the grandest charge that was ever made by mortal man."[176] Although he ordered his subordinate commanders to walk during the charge, Barksdale himself rode on horseback "in front, leading the way, hat off, his wispy hair shining so that it reminded [a Confederate staff officer] of 'the white plume of Navarre'."[177]

The Confederates smashed the brigade manning the Peach Orchard line, wounding and capturing the Union brigade commander himself. Some of Barksdale's regiments turned to the north and shattered Maj. Gen. Andrew A. Humphreys's division. Others of his regiments went straight ahead. By the time his men had gone as far as Plum Run, a mile into the assault, they were counterattacked by a brigade under Colonel George L. Willard. Barksdale was wounded in his left knee, followed by a cannonball to his left foot, and finally was hit by another bullet to his chest, knocking him off his horse. He told his aide, W.R. Boyd, "I am killed! Tell my wife and children that I died fighting at my post."[178] His troops were forced to leave him for dead on the field and he died the next morning in a Union field hospital (the Joseph Hummelbaugh farmhouse).

Barksdale's remains were interred in the Barksdale family plot of Greenwood Cemetery, Jackson, Mississippi with no marker, but he has cenotaphs in both Greenwood Cemetery and in Friendship Cemetery, Columbus, Mississippi.

In popular media

Barksdale is portrayed in the film *Gettysburg* and in the prequel, *Gods and Generals*, by Lester Kinsolving, who is a relative of Barksdale.

Barksdale is also featured in the 2011 History Channel film *Gettysburg*.

The streets in the Potomac Crossing subdivision in Leesburg, Virginia, are named (in part) after the regimental commanders of the Battle of Ball's Bluff

(October 21, 1861). Barksdale Drive was named for Col. Barksdale and is the primary east-west conduit in the development, running just short of a mile to either end of the neighborhood.

References

- Clark, Champ, and the Editors of Time-Life Books. *Gettysburg: The Confederate High Tide*. Alexandria, VA: Time-Life Books, 1985. <templatestyles src="Module:Citation/CS1/styles.css" />ISBN 0-8094-4758-4.
- Eicher, John H., and David J. Eicher. *Civil War High Commands*. Stanford, CA: Stanford University Press, 2001. <templatestyles src="Module:Citation/CS1/styles.css" />ISBN 0-8047-3641-3.
- Pfanz, Harry W. *Gettysburg – The Second Day*. Chapel Hill: University of North Carolina Press, 1987. <templatestyles src="Module:Citation/CS1/styles.css" />ISBN 0-8078-1749-X.
- Tagg, Larry. *The Generals of Gettysburg*[179]. Campbell, CA: Savas Publishing, 1998. <templatestyles src="Module:Citation/CS1/styles.css" />ISBN 1-882810-30-9.
- Tucker, Phillip T. *Barksdale's Charge: The True High Tide of the Confederacy at Gettysburg, July 2, 1863*. Casemate Publishers, 2013. <templatestyles src="Module:Citation/CS1/styles.css" />ISBN 9781612001791.
- Warner, Ezra J. *Generals in Gray: Lives of the Confederate Commanders*. Baton Rouge: Louisiana State University Press, 1959. <templatestyles src="Module:Citation/CS1/styles.css" />ISBN 0-8071-0823-5.
- U.S. Congress Biographical Directory[180]

Further reading

- Guelzo, Allen C. *Gettysburg: The Last Invasion*. New York: Knopf, 2013. <templatestyles src="Module:Citation/CS1/styles.css" />ISBN 0-3075-9408-4.
- His Gallant Spirit Went Home: The Burial of General William Barksdale in Jackson[181] Mississippians in the Confederate Army, 2013.

U.S. House of Representatives		
Preceded by *Vacant*	**Member of the U.S. House of Representatives from Mississippi's at-large congressional district** 1853 – 1855	Succeeded by *District established*

William Dorsey Pender

William Dorsey Pender	
Born	February 6, 1834 Edgecombe County, North Carolina
Died	July 18, 1863 (aged 29) Staunton, Virginia
Place of burial	Calvary Church Cemetery Tarboro, North Carolina
Allegiance	United States of America Confederate States of America
Service/<wbr/>branch	United States Army Confederate States Army
Years of service	1854–61 (USA) 1861–63 (CSA)
Rank	First Lieutenant (USA) Major General (CSA)
Commands held	3rd North Carolina Infantry 6th North Carolina Infantry Pender's Brigade Pender's Division, III Corps, Army of Northern Virginia
Battles/wars	Indian Wars American Civil War • Battle of Seven Pines • Seven Days Battles • Battle of Cedar Mountain • Second Battle of Manassas • Battle of Harpers Ferry • Battle of Sharpsburg • Battle of Fredericksburg • Battle of Chancellorsville • Battle of Gettysburg (DOW)

Relations	Robert R. Bridgers (Cousin)
	Mary Francis "Fanny" Sheppard (Wife)
	Samuel Turner Pender (Son)
	William Dorsey Pender, Jr. (Son)
	David Pender (Brother)

William Dorsey Pender (February 6, 1834 – July 18, 1863) was a General in the Confederacy in the American Civil War serving as a Brigade and Divisional commander. Promoted to brigadier on the battlefield at Seven Pines by Confederate President Jefferson Davis in person, he fought in the Seven Days Battles and at Second Manassas, Fredericksburg and Chancellorsville, being wounded in each of these engagements. Lee rated him as one of the most promising of his commanders,[182] promoting him to major general at twenty-nine. Pender was mortally wounded on the second day of Gettysburg.

Early life

Dorsey Pender, as he was known to his friends, was born on February 6, 1834, at Pender's Crossroads, Edgecombe County, North Carolina to James and Sally Routh Pender, the youngest of four children, with two brothers and a sister. His father was a planter who owned more than 500 acres and twenty-one slaves in the vicinity of Tarboro, making the family a member of the local elite. Though descended from Virginians, Pender's parents were longtime residents of Edgecombe County. He spent his youth on the farm, hunting, fishing, and riding, before becoming a teenaged clerk in the Tarboro store owned by his older brother Robert.[183]

He graduated from the United States Military Academy in 1854, nineteenth out of 46 in his class, and was commissioned a second lieutenant in the 2nd U.S. Artillery.[184] He served later in the 1st Dragoons (heavy cavalry), where he demonstrated personal bravery in Washington Territory, fighting in the Indian Wars.

Civil War

On March 21, 1861, Pender resigned from the U.S. Army and was appointed a captain of artillery in the Confederate States Army. By May he was a colonel in command of the 3rd North Carolina Infantry (also designated the 13th North Carolina) and then the 6th North Carolina. Tried in combat successfully in the Battle of Seven Pines in June 1862, he was promoted to brigadier general and command of a brigade of North Carolinians in Maj. Gen. A.P. Hill's *Light Division*. Confederate President Jefferson Davis personally promoted Pender on the Seven Pines battlefield.

During the Seven Days Battles, Pender was an aggressive brigade commander. He was wounded in the arm at the Battle of Glendale, but recovered quickly enough to rejoin his brigade and fight at Cedar Mountain, Second Manassas (where he received a minor head wound from an exploding shell), Harpers Ferry, and Battle of Sharpsburg. At Sharpsburg, Pender arrived in the nick of time with A.P. Hill after a 17-mile march to save the Army of Northern Virginia from serious defeat on its right flank.

At Fredericksburg, he was wounded again, in his left arm, but the bone was unbroken, so he continued in command, despite the spectacle of him riding around bleeding. At Chancellorsville, on May 2, 1863, A.P. Hill was wounded in Thomas "Stonewall" Jackson's famous march and attack on the flank of the Union XI Corps; Pender assumed command of the division. On the following day, Pender was wounded in the arm yet again, this time a minor injury from a spent bullet that had killed an officer who stood in front of him.

Following the death of Jackson, Gen. Robert E. Lee reorganized his army and promoted A.P. Hill to command the newly formed Third Corps. Pender, at the young age of 29, was promoted to major general and division command. He was well regarded by his superiors. Lee wrote to Jefferson Davis, "Pender is an excellent officer, attentive, industrious and brave; has been conspicuous in every battle, and, I believe, wounded in almost all of them."[185]

Death

Dorsey Pender's promising career ended at the Battle of Gettysburg. On July 1, 1863, his division moved in support of Maj. Gen. Henry Heth's division down the Chambersburg Pike towards Gettysburg. Heth encountered stronger resistance from the Union I Corps than he expected and was repulsed in his first assault. Uncharacteristically for the normally aggressive Pender, he did not immediately charge in to assist Heth, but took up positions on Herr Ridge and awaited developments. In Heth's second assault of the day, Hill ordered Pender to support Heth, but Heth declined the assistance and Pender once again kept his division in the rear. For the second time in the day, Heth got more than he bargained for in his assault on McPherson's Ridge. He was wounded in action and could not request the assistance from Pender he had earlier refused. Hill ordered Pender to attack the new Union position on Seminary Ridge at about 4 p.m. The 30-minute assault by three of his brigades was very bloody and the brigade of Brig. Gen. Alfred M. Scales was almost completely destroyed by Union artillery canister fire. In the end, Pender's men forced the Union troops back in and through Gettysburg.

On July 2, Pender was posted near the Lutheran Seminary. During the *en echelon* attack that started with James Longstreet's assault on the right, from the Round Tops through the Peach Orchard, Pender's division was to continue in the attack sequence near Cemetery Hill, to the left of Maj. Gen. Richard H. Anderson's attack on Cemetery Ridge. Pender was wounded in the thigh by a shell fragment fired from Cemetery Hill, and turned command over to Brig. Gen. James H. Lane. His division's momentum was broken by the change in command and no effective assault was completed. Pender was evacuated to Staunton, Virginia, where an artery in his leg ruptured on July 18. Surgeons amputated his leg in an attempt to save him, but he died a few hours later.[186]

His superiors wrote in their official reports of the Gettysburg Campaign about Pender's death:

```
<templatestyles src="Template:Quote/styles.css"/>
```

The loss of Major-General Pender is severely felt by the army and the country. He served with this army from the beginning of the war, and took a distinguished part in all its engagements. Wounded on several occasions, he never left his command in action until he received the injury that resulted in his death. His promise and usefulness as an officer were only equaled by the purity and excellence of his private life.[187]

—*Robert E. Lee*

```
<templatestyles src="Template:Quote/styles.css"/>
```

On this day (July 2, 1863), also, the Confederacy lost the invaluable services of Major General W. D. Pender, wounded by a shell, and since dead. No man fell during this bloody battle of Gettysburg more regretted than he, nor around whose youthful brow were clustered brighter rays of glory.[188]

—*A.P. Hill*

Legacy

He is buried in the graveyard at Calvary Episcopal Church, Tarboro, North Carolina. He is memorialized in the name of Pender County, North Carolina, founded in 1875. He is the posthumous author of *The General to his Lady: The Civil War letters of William Dorsey Pender to Fanny Pender*, published in 1965.

During World War II, the United States Navy commissioned a Liberty Ship, the SS *William D. Pender*, in honor of the fallen general.

References

- Eicher, John H., and David J. Eicher, *Civil War High Commands*. Stanford: Stanford University Press, 2001. <templatestyles src="Module:Citation/CS1/styles.css" />ISBN 978-0-8047-3641-1.
- Longacre, Edward G. *General William Dorsey Pender: A Military Biography*. Da Capo Press, 2001. <templatestyles src="Module:Citation/CS1/styles.css" />ISBN 978-1580970341.
- Sifakis, Stewart. *Who Was Who in the Civil War*. New York: Facts On File, 1988. <templatestyles src="Module:Citation/CS1/styles.css" />ISBN 978-0-8160-1055-4.
- Tagg, Larry. *The Generals of Gettysburg*[189]. Campbell, CA: Savas Publishing, 1998. <templatestyles src="Module:Citation/CS1/styles.css" />ISBN 1-882810-30-9.
- U.S. War Department. *The War of the Rebellion*[190]: *a Compilation of the Official Records of the Union and Confederate Armies*. Washington, DC: U.S. Government Printing Office, 1880–1901.
- Warner, Ezra J. *Generals in Gray: Lives of the Confederate Commanders*. Baton Rouge: Louisiana State University Press, 1959. <templatestyles src="Module:Citation/CS1/styles.css" />ISBN 978-0-8071-0823-9.
- Wills, Brian Steel, *Confederate General William Dorsey Pender*. Baton Rouge: Louisiana State University Press, 2013. <templatestyles src="Module:Citation/CS1/styles.css" />ISBN 978-0-8071-5299-7

External links

- "William Dorsey Pender"[191]. Find a Grave. Retrieved August 14, 2010.<templatestyles src="Module:Citation/CS1/styles.css"></templatestyles>
- Pender's papers at the Southern Historical Collection[192]

Paul Jones Semmes

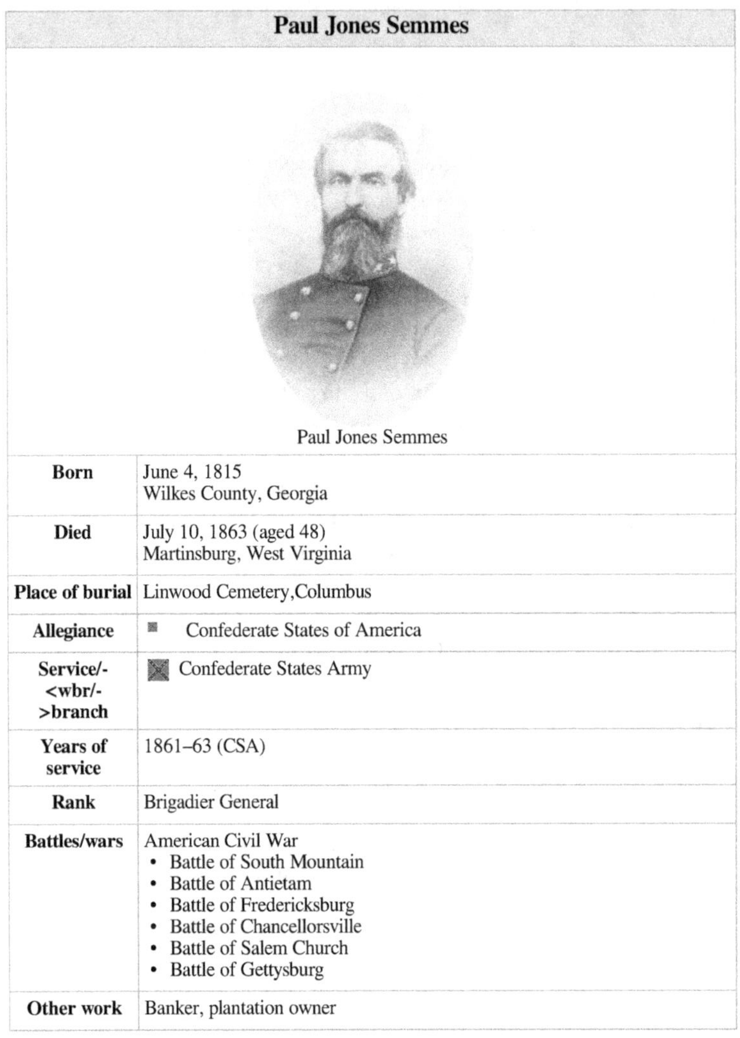

Paul Jones Semmes	
	Paul Jones Semmes
Born	June 4, 1815 Wilkes County, Georgia
Died	July 10, 1863 (aged 48) Martinsburg, West Virginia
Place of burial	Linwood Cemetery,Columbus
Allegiance	Confederate States of America
Service/-<wbr/->branch	Confederate States Army
Years of service	1861–63 (CSA)
Rank	Brigadier General
Battles/wars	American Civil War • Battle of South Mountain • Battle of Antietam • Battle of Fredericksburg • Battle of Chancellorsville • Battle of Salem Church • Battle of Gettysburg
Other work	Banker, plantation owner

Paul Jones Semmes (June 4, 1815 – July 10, 1863) was a banker, business-
man, and a Confederate brigadier general in the American Civil War, mortally
wounded at the Battle of Gettysburg.

Early life

Semmes was born at Montford's Plantation in Wilkes County, Georgia.[193] He was a cousin of future Confederate naval hero, *CSS Alabama* Captain Raphael Semmes. His half-brother, Albert Gallatin Semmes, later became an Associate Justice of the Florida Supreme Court. Paul Semmes was educated at the Beman School in Hancock County. He attended the University of Virginia and became a banker and planter in Wilkes County, Georgia.[194] He was elected commander of the Georgia Militia 1st Brigade of the 4th Division in 1837 and held that commission until 1840 when he moved to Columbus, Georgia.[195] His business endeavors flourished and he became one of Columbus's most prominent citizens. From 1846 to 1861, he served as a captain in the Georgia militia. He was the author of the 1855 manual, *Infantry Tactics*. In 1860, Governor Joseph E. Brown appointed Semmes as quartermaster general for the state and authorized him to handle all military purchases. In August 1860 Semmes was appointed Brigadier General of the Knights of the Golden Circle.[196]

Civil War

After the start of the Civil War, Semmes was appointed colonel of the 2nd Georgia Infantry. He was promoted to brigadier general on March 11, 1862.[197] During the Peninsula Campaign, he was a brigade commander in Brig. Gen. John B. Magruder's Corps in the defense of Richmond. Rushed northward at the start of the Maryland Campaign, Semmes's brigade rejoined the Army of Northern Virginia in the division of Maj. Gen. Lafayette McLaws just as it was entering Maryland. His men participated in the holding action at Crampton's Gap during the Battle of South Mountain. At Sharpsburg, Semmes's brigade was a key part of General McLaws's strong counterattack that stunned the Union II Corps. In early November, his brigade was reorganized so that it only contained Georgia regiments. Held in reserve at the Battle of Fredericksburg, Semmes's reconstituted brigade served well at Chancellorsville, where it blunted the advance of an entire VI Corps division, and at Salem Church.

Death and legacy

Semmes was mortally wounded in the thigh while leading a charge across the Wheatfield at the Battle of Gettysburg on July 2, 1863. He died eight days later in Martinsburg, West Virginia, and was buried in Linwood Cemetery (Columbus, Georgia). Shortly before his death, Semmes told a war correspondent, "I consider it a privilege to die for my country." The last letter that he wrote to his wife may be seen in the online collection of the Gilder Lehrman Institute of American History[198].

General Robert E. Lee lamented Semmes's untimely loss, writing that he "died as he had lived, discharging the highest duty of a patriot with devotion that never faltered and courage that shrank from no danger."

References

- Eicher, John H., and David J. Eicher, *Civil War High Commands*. Stanford: Stanford University Press, 2001. <templatestyles src="Module:Citation/CS1/styles.css" />ISBN 978-0-8047-3641-1.
- Evans, Clement A., ed. *Confederate Military History: A Library of Confederate States History*[199]. 12 vols. Atlanta: Confederate Publishing Company, 1899. <templatestyles src="Module:Citation/CS1/styles.css" />OCLC 833588[200].
- Sifakis, Stewart. *Who Was Who in the Civil War*. New York: Facts On File, 1988. <templatestyles src="Module:Citation/CS1/styles.css" />ISBN 978-0-8160-1055-4.
- Warner, Ezra J. *Generals in Gray: Lives of the Confederate Commanders*. Baton Rouge: Louisiana State University Press, 1959. <templatestyles src="Module:Citation/CS1/styles.css" />ISBN 978-0-8071-0823-9.
- Smith, Gordon Burns, *History of the Georgia Militia, 1783-1861, Volume One, Campaigns and Generals*, Milledgeville: Boyd Publishing, 2000. ASIN:B003L1PRKI.

Further reading

- Pfanz, Harry W. *Gettysburg – The Second Day*. Chapel Hill: University of North Carolina Press, 1987. <templatestyles src="Module:Citation/CS1/styles.css" />ISBN 0-8078-1749-X.
- Keehn, David C. "Knights of the Golden Circle". Baton Rouge: Louisiana State University Press, 2013. <templatestyles src="Module:Citation/CS1/styles.css" />ISBN 978-0-8071-5004-7* Machowski & White "Chancellorsville's Forgotten Front" El Dorado Hills Savas Beatie <templatestyles src="Module:Citation/CS1/styles.css" />ISBN 978-1-61121-136-8,

External links

- "Paul Jones Semmes"[201]. Find a Grave. Retrieved 2008-02-13.<templatestyles src="Module:Citation/CS1/styles.css"></templatestyles>
- Sheet music for a Requiem in Honor of Paul J. Semmes[202]
- The burial of Paul J. Semmes[203]

Stephen H. Weed

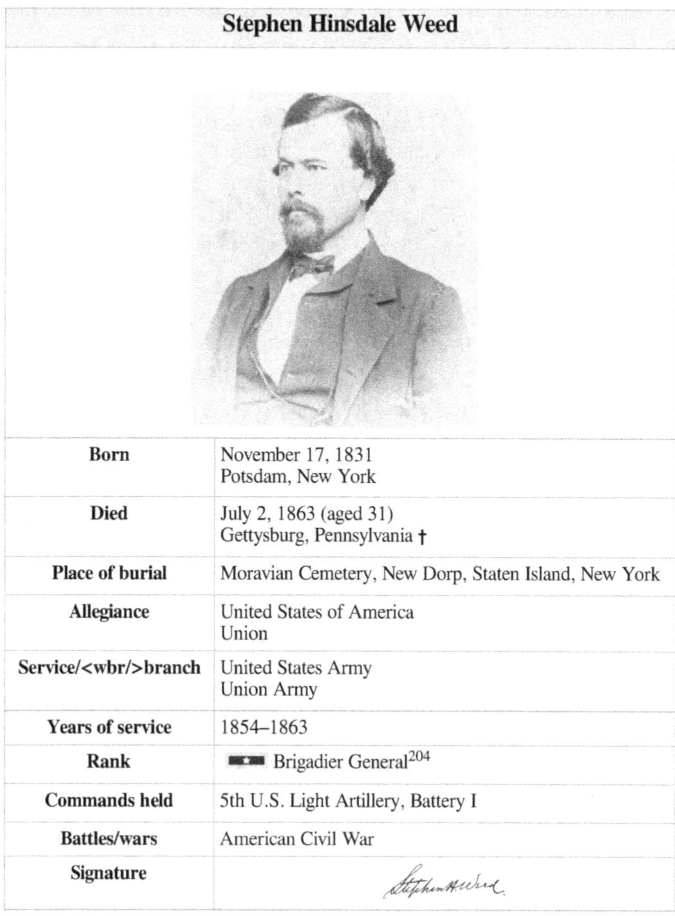

Stephen Hinsdale Weed	
Born	November 17, 1831 Potsdam, New York
Died	July 2, 1863 (aged 31) Gettysburg, Pennsylvania †
Place of burial	Moravian Cemetery, New Dorp, Staten Island, New York
Allegiance	United States of America Union
Service/<wbr/>branch	United States Army Union Army
Years of service	1854–1863
Rank	Brigadier General[204]
Commands held	5th U.S. Light Artillery, Battery I
Battles/wars	American Civil War
Signature	

Stephen Hinsdale Weed (November 17, 1831 – July 2, 1863) was a career military officer in the United States Army. He was killed defending Little Round Top during the Battle of Gettysburg in the American Civil War.

Early life and career

Weed was born in Potsdam, New York, the second of four children born to John Kilbourne and Charity Winslow Weed. He was appointed to the United States Military Academy, graduating 27th of 46 students in the Class of 1854. Among his classmates were ten other future Civil War generals, including

Oliver O. Howard and J.E.B. Stuart. He received a brevet rank of second lieutenant and was assigned to the 2nd U.S. Artillery on July 1, 1854. He served on frontier duty in Texas. In December, he received his regular rank of second lieutenant in the 4th U.S. Artillery.

Two years later, he was promoted to first lieutenant and fought in Florida in the Seminole Wars in 1856–57. He was engaged in quelling the Kansas disturbances in 1858. By now a combat veteran commanding Battery B, 4th U.S. Artillery, he participated in the Utah War, helping restore order to the territory. He saw action again fighting Indians at the Battle of Egan Station in the Utah Territory[205] on August 11, 1860, and at the Battle of Deep Creek on September 6, 1860.

Civil War

With the outbreak of the Civil War, Weed was promoted captain of the newly formed Battery I, 5th U.S. Artillery in May 1861. He remained at Camp Curtin in Harrisburg, Pennsylvania, training his crews until the spring of 1862, when they served in the Peninsula Campaign and at Second Bull Run. He commanded his battery during the fierce artillery duel at Antietam. Promoted to command of all the artillery of the V Corps, his guns were in action at the Battle of Fredericksburg. From December 1862 through January 1863, he was stationed at Falmouth, Virginia. After a short leave of absence, he took part in the Battle of Chancellorsville, commanding the artillery of the 2nd Division, V Corps. On June 6, 1863, Weed left the regular army artillery to accept a commission as a brigadier general in the volunteer army. He was assigned command of 3rd Brigade in the 2nd Division, V Corps.

At Gettysburg, his brigade went to the relief of Col. Strong Vincent's brigade on Little Round Top. His vanguard repelled a Confederate attack that had outflanked Vincent's right. Col. Patrick O'Rorke of the 140th New York Infantry was killed leading that counterattack. Elements of Weed's brigade helped move the guns of Lt. Charles E. Hazlett's Battery D, 5th United States Artillery to the top of the hill. Weed was mortally wounded in the chest (possibly by a sharpshooter hidden in Devil's Den) while standing near these guns. His last words were reported as "I would rather die here than that the rebels should gain an inch of this ground." Lt. Hazlett was killed trying to hear what Weed was saying. Command of the brigade fell to Col. Kenner Garrard of the 146th New York Infantry.

According to Tillie Pierce, a young girl from Gettysburg who witnessed the horrors of the battle from the Weikert farm on Taneytown Road just to the east of Little Round Top, Weed died in the Weikert's "basement", which served as the "cellar-kitchen." Not knowing who the man was, Tillie watched over him briefly while an attending soldier stepped away, whereupon she asked "the wounded soldier" if there was anything she could do for him: "Will you promise to come back in the morning to see me," he asked. She promised to do so, and, as she got up to leave for the night, Weed reminded, "Now don't you forget your promise." The next morning, she "hastened down to the little basement room," but "the soldier lay there – dead. His faithful attendant was still at his side." As she "stood there gazing in sadness at the prostrate form, the attendant looked up . . . and asked: 'Do you know who this is?" When she said no, he replied, "This is the body of General Weed; a New York man."[206]

Weed's body was returned home and buried in the Moravian Cemetery in New Dorp, a village on Staten Island in Richmond County, New York.

In memoriam

Redoubt A of the military defenses around Washington, D.C., was renamed "Fort Weed" in September 1863 in his memory. Following the war, Post #91 of the Grand Army of the Republic in New York City was named the Stephen H. Weed Post. In 1902, Army General Orders No. 16 renamed a portion of Fort Wadsworth along The Narrows in New York Harbor as Battery Weed. In 1930, a street in New Dorp Beach, Staten Island was named Weed Avenue, dedicated to Stephen H. Weed.

References

- Eicher, John H., and David J. Eicher. *Civil War High Commands*. Stanford, CA: Stanford University Press, 2001. <templatestyles src="Module:Citation/CS1/styles.css" />ISBN 0-8047-3641-3.
- Heitman, Francis B. *Historical Register and Dictionary of the United States Army; From Its Organization, September 29, 1789, to March 2, 1903*. 2 vols. Urbana: University of Illinois Press, 1963. <templatestyles src="Module:Citation/CS1/styles.css" />ISBN 0-942211-73-1. First published 1903 by U.S. Government Printing Office.
- Warner, Ezra J. *Generals in Blue: Lives of the Union Commanders*. Baton Rouge: Louisiana State University Press, 1964. <templatestyles src="Module:Citation/CS1/styles.css" />ISBN 0-8071-0822-7.
- Alleman, Matilda "Tillie" Pierce, *At Gettysburg, or, What a Girl Saw and Heard of the Battle. A True Narrative.*[207] New York, W. Lake Borland, 1889. <templatestyles src="Module:Citation/CS1/styles.css" />ISBN 0-935523-07-3.

External links

- Stephen H. Weed[208] at Find a Grave

Samuel K. Zook

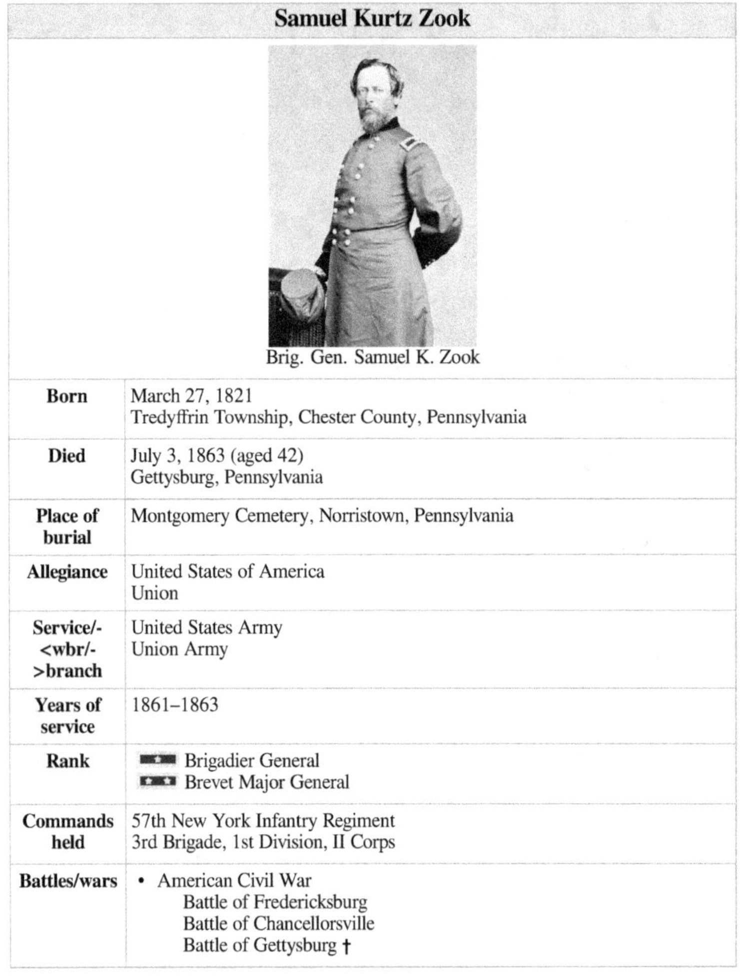

Samuel Kurtz Zook	
	Brig. Gen. Samuel K. Zook
Born	March 27, 1821 Tredyffrin Township, Chester County, Pennsylvania
Died	July 3, 1863 (aged 42) Gettysburg, Pennsylvania
Place of burial	Montgomery Cemetery, Norristown, Pennsylvania
Allegiance	United States of America Union
Service/-<wbr/->branch	United States Army Union Army
Years of service	1861–1863
Rank	Brigadier General Brevet Major General
Commands held	57th New York Infantry Regiment 3rd Brigade, 1st Division, II Corps
Battles/wars	• American Civil War Battle of Fredericksburg Battle of Chancellorsville Battle of Gettysburg †

Samuel Kosciuszko Zook (born **Samuel Kurtz Zook**, March 27, 1821 – July 3, 1863) was a Union general during the American Civil War, mortally wounded in action during the Battle of Gettysburg.

Early years

Zook was born in Tredyffrin, Chester County, Pennsylvania. His parents were David and Eleanor Stephens Zook and his paternal ancestors were of the Mennonite faith. At an early age, he moved with his parents to the home of his maternal grandmother at Valley Forge and the tradition of George Washington's winter encampment there during the American Revolutionary War fueled a lifelong interest in military matters. His father, David Zook, had been a major during the American Revolution, further fueling his interests.[209] From the time he was old enough to carry a musket, he participated in local militia activities. At the age of 19, he became a lieutenant in the Pennsylvania militia and the adjutant of the 100th[210] or 110th[211] Pennsylvania regiment.

Zook entered the emerging field of telegraphy, became a proficient operator, and worked on crews to string wires as far west as the Mississippi River. He moved to New York City in 1846[212] or 1851 and became the superintendent of the Washington and New York Telegraph Company. He made several discoveries in electric science that gave him reputation. In New York City, he also joined the 6th New York Governor's Guard (militia) regiment and had achieved the rank of lieutenant colonel by the time the Civil War broke out.

Civil War

The 6th New York Militia helped out as a 90-day regiment during the first summer of the war. Zook served as the military governor in Annapolis, seeking support from politically influential men there to achieve a regimental command of his own. After he was mustered out, he raised the 57th New York Infantry (National Guard Rifles) and became its colonel on October 19, 1861.

Zook's first combat was during the Seven Days Battles of 1862. His regiment was assigned to William H. French's brigade in Edwin V. Sumner's division of the Army of the Potomac, under Maj. Gen. George B. McClellan. Zook was personally scouting far out in front of his regiment in the run-up to the Battle of Gaines' Mill, got behind enemy lines, and found that Confederate Maj. Gen. John B. Magruder was conducting an elaborate deception, making it appear that he had significantly more troops in his sector than he actually had. Zook's discovery was reported up to McClellan, but it was ignored, and Union troops that could have been used successfully elsewhere remain tied down.

Figure 42: *General Samuel K. Zook*

Fredericksburg

Zook was forced to go on medical leave, probably due to chronic and disabling rheumatism, thus missing the Battle of Antietam. When he returned to the Army he was given command of French's brigade (3rd Brigade, 1st Division, II Corps) under division commander Maj. Gen. Winfield S. Hancock. The brigade was one of the first to arrive at Fredericksburg, Virginia, and he wanted to cross over the Rappahannock River as quickly as possible, before Confederate General Robert E. Lee could reinforce the town and the heights beyond it. However, Army of the Potomac commander Maj. Gen. Ambrose Burnside prevented the movement, wanting to wait for his army to concentrate and to receive pontoon bridges to make the river crossing. Zook wrote on December 10, "If we had had the pontoons promised when we arrived here we could have the hills on the other side of the river without cost over 50 men—now it will cost at least 10,000 if not more." While waiting for the pontoons to arrive, Zook served as military governor of Falmouth, Virginia.

When the Battle of Fredericksburg began in earnest on December 13, French's division was the first to assault Marye's Heights. After being repulsed with heavy losses, Hancock's division moved forward with Zook's brigade in the lead. Zook had his horse shot out from under him and was momentarily stunned, but managed to lead his men to within 60 yards of the Stone Wall, one of the farthest Union advances of the battle. His brigade suffered 527 of the 12,000 Union casualties that night. General Hancock praised Zook's attack for its "spirit". Zook wrote afterward, "Now by God, if I don't get my star, I'm coming home." He was promoted to brigadier general in March 1863, to rank from November 29, 1862.[213] Despite his successful promotion, however, the battle of Fredericksburg affected him deeply:

<templatestyles src="Template:Quote/styles.css"/>

> *I walked over the field, close under the enemy's picket line, last night about 3 o'clock. The ground was strewn thickly with corpses of the hero's who perished there on Saturday. I never realized before what war was. I never before felt so horribly since I was born. To see men dashed to pieces by shot & torn into shreds by shells during the heat and crash of battle is bad enough God knows, but to walk alone amongst slaughtered brave in the "still small hours" of the night would make the bravest man living "blue". God grant I may never have to repeat my last night's experience.*

> *—Samuel K. Zook, letter to E. I. Wade, December 16, 1862*

At the Battle of Chancellorsville in May 1863, Zook's brigade fought in the defensive line around the Chancellor Mansion, but facing east, where combat was lighter and his men suffered only 188 casualties. Disabled again by rheumatism, he left on medical leave to Washington, D.C., and rejoined his brigade at the end of June to march into Pennsylvania for the Gettysburg Campaign.

Gettysburg

On July 2, 1863, the second day of the Battle of Gettysburg, Brig. Gen. John C. Caldwell's division, including Zook's brigade, was sent to reinforce the crumbling III Corps line that was being assaulted by the Confederate corps of Lt. Gen. James Longstreet. Zook was directed by one of the III Corps staff officers toward the Wheatfield to reinforce the brigade of Col. Régis de Trobriand and to fill a gap near the Stony Hill. Zook, on horseback, led his men up the hill, which attracted the attention of men from the advancing 3rd and 7th South Carolina Infantry regiments, of Joseph B. Kershaw's brigade. He was struck by rifle fire in the shoulder, chest, and abdomen, and taken behind the lines for medical treatment at a toll house on the Baltimore Pike. He died from his wounds on July 3 and is buried near the grave of General Winfield Scott Hancock in Montgomery Cemetery in West Norriton Township, Montgomery County, Pennsylvania, near Norristown, Pennsylvania. He received a brevet promotion to major general for Gettysburg, awarded as of July 2. A small monument near the Wheatfield Road commemorates Zook's death.[214]

One of his soldiers in the 57th New York later characterized Zook as "a good disciplinarian; he hated cowardice and shams; had no patience with a man

Figure 43: *Zook Monument, The Wheatfield, Gettysburg Battlefield.*

that neglected duty; was blunt, somewhat severe, yet good hearted ... a born soldier, quick of intellect, and absolutely without fear."[215]

References

- Eicher, John H., and David J. Eicher. *Civil War High Commands*. Stanford, CA: Stanford University Press, 2001. <templatestyles src="Module:Citation/CS1/styles.css" />ISBN 0-8047-3641-3.
- Gambone, A. M. *"... If tomorrow night finds me dead..." The Life of General Samuel K. Zook*. Army of the Potomac series. Baltimore: Butternut and Blue, 1996. <templatestyles src="Module:Citation/CS1/styles.css" />ISBN 0-935523-53-7.
- New York (State), William F. Fox, and Daniel Edgar Sickles. New York at Gettysburg: Final Report on the Battlefield of Gettysburg[216]. Albany, NY: J. B. Lyon Company, 1900. <templatestyles src="Module:Citation/CS1/styles.css" />OCLC 607395975[217].
- Tagg, Larry. *The Generals of Gettysburg*[218]. Campbell, CA: Savas Publishing, 1998. <templatestyles src="Module:Citation/CS1/styles.css" />ISBN 1-882810-30-9.

- Warner, Ezra J. *Generals in Blue: Lives of the Union Commanders*. Baton Rouge: Louisiana State University Press, 1964. <templatestyles src="Module:Citation/CS1/styles.css" />ISBN 0-8071-0822-7.

External links

- Media related to Samuel K. Zook at Wikimedia Commons

Killed: Day 3 - July 3rd, 1863

Lewis Armistead

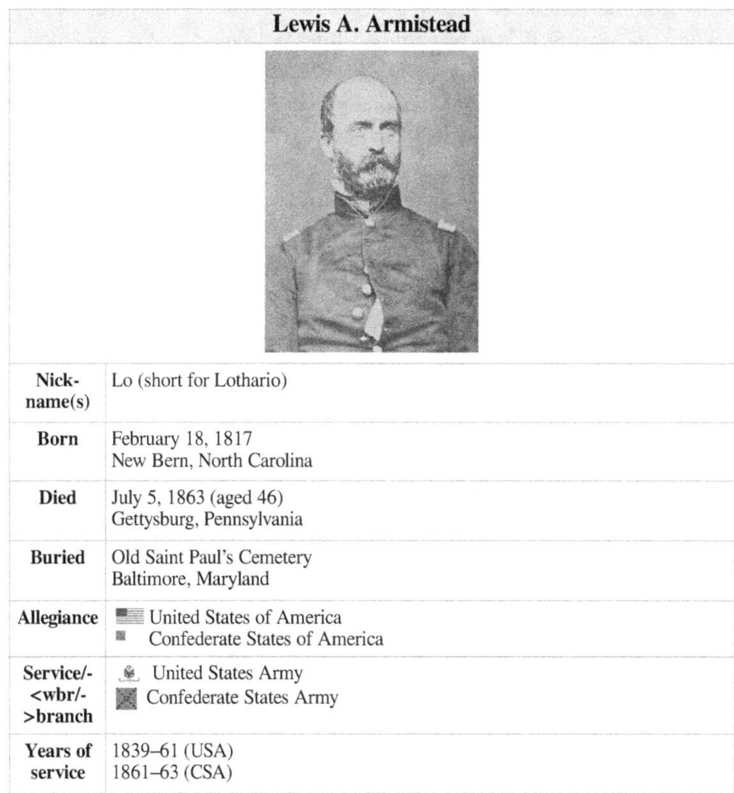

Lewis A. Armistead	
Nickname(s)	Lo (short for Lothario)
Born	February 18, 1817 New Bern, North Carolina
Died	July 5, 1863 (aged 46) Gettysburg, Pennsylvania
Buried	Old Saint Paul's Cemetery Baltimore, Maryland
Allegiance	United States of America Confederate States of America
Service/-<wbr/->branch	United States Army Confederate States Army
Years of service	1839–61 (USA) 1861–63 (CSA)

Rank	Brevet Major (USA) Brigadier General (CSA)
Unit	6th U.S. Infantry
Commands held	57th Virginia Infantry Armistead's Bde, Pickett's Div, I Corps

Battles/-wars	Mexican–American War
	• Battle of Chapultepec
	Mohave War
	• Battle of the Colorado River
	American Civil War
	• Battle of Seven Pines
	• Seven Days Battles
	  • Battle of Malvern Hill
	• Second Battle of Bull Run
	• Battle of Antietam
	• Battle of Fredericksburg
	• Battle of Gettysburg
	  • Pickett's Charge †

Lewis Addison Armistead (February 18, 1817 – July 5, 1863) was a career United States Army officer who became a brigadier general in the Confederate States Army during the American Civil War. On July 3, 1863, as part of Pickett's Charge during the Battle of Gettysburg, Armistead led his brigade to the farthest point reached by Confederate forces during the charge, a point now referred to as the high-water mark of the Confederacy. However, he and his men were overwhelmed, and he was wounded and captured by Union troops. He died in a field hospital two days later.

Early life

Armistead, known to friends as "Lo" (for *Lothario*),[219] was born in the home of his great-grandfather, John Wright Stanly, in New Bern, North Carolina, to Walker Keith Armistead and Elizabeth Stanly. He came from an esteemed military family.[220] Armistead was of entirely English descent, and all of his ancestry had been in Virginia since the early 1600s.[221] The first of his ancestors to emigrate to North America was William Armistead from Yorkshire, England.[222] Armistead's father was one of five brothers who fought in the War of 1812; another was Major George Armistead, the commander of Fort McHenry during the battle that inspired Francis Scott Key to write "The Star-Spangled Banner", which would later become the national anthem of the United States. On his mother's side, his grandfather John Stanly was a U.S. Congressman, and his uncle Edward Stanly served as military governor of eastern North Carolina during the Civil War.

Armistead attended the United States Military Academy, but resigned following an incident in which he broke a plate over the head of fellow cadet (and future Confederate general) Jubal Early.[223] He was also having academic difficulties, however, particularly in French (a subject of difficulty for many West Point cadets of that era), and some historians cite academic failure as his true reason for leaving the academy.[224]

His influential father managed to obtain for his son a second lieutenant's commission in the 6th U.S. Infantry on July 10, 1839, at roughly the time his classmates graduated. He was promoted to first lieutenant on March 30, 1844. Armistead's first marriage was to Cecelia Lee Love, a distant cousin of Robert E. Lee, in 1844.[225] They had two children: Walker Keith Armistead and Flora Lee Armistead.

Armistead then served in Fort Towson, Arkansas, Fort Washita near the Oklahoma border. Serving in the Mexican War, he was appointed brevet captain for Contreras and Churubusco, wounded at Chapultepec, and was appointed a brevet major for Molino del Rey and Chapultepec.

Armistead continued in the Army after the Mexican War, assigned in 1849 to recruiting duty in Kentucky, where he was diagnosed with a severe case of erysipelas, but he later recovered. In April 1850, the Armisteads lost their little girl, Flora Love, at Jefferson Barracks. Armistead was posted to Fort Dodge, but in the winter he had to take his wife Cecelia to Mobile, Alabama, where she died December 12, 1850, from an unknown cause. He returned to Fort Dodge. In 1852 the Armistead family home in Virginia burned, destroying nearly everything. Armistead took leave in October 1852 to go home and help his family. While on leave Armistead married his second wife, the widow Cornelia Taliaferro Jamison, in Alexandria, Virginia, on March 17, 1853.Wikipedia:Citation needed They both went west when Armistead returned to duty shortly thereafter.

The new Armistead family traveled from post to post in Nebraska, Missouri, and Kansas. The couple had one child, Lewis B. Armistead, who died on December 6, 1854, and was also buried at Jefferson Barracks next to Flora Lee Armistead. He was promoted to captain on March 3, 1855.[226] His second wife, Cornelia Taliaferro Jamison, died on August 3, 1855, at Fort Riley, Kansas, during a cholera epidemic.Wikipedia:Citation needed

Between 1855 and 1858 Armistead served at posts on the Smokey Hill River in Kansas Territory, Bent's Fort, Pole Creek, Laramie River, and Republican Fork of the Kansas River in Nebraska Territory. In 1858, his 6th Infantry Regiment was sent as part of the reinforcements sent to Utah in the aftermath of the Utah War. Not being required there, they were sent to California with the intention of sending them on to Washington Territory. However, a Mohave attack on civilians on the Beale Wagon Road diverted his regiment to the southern deserts along the Colorado River to participate in The Mojave Expedition of 1858-59.

Lt. Col. William Hoffman, at the head of a column of six companies of infantry, two of dragoons, and some artillery, struggled up the Colorado River from Fort Yuma. On April 23, 1859, Colonel Hoffman dictated a peace to the overawed Mohave chiefs, threatening annihilation to the tribe if they did not cease hostilities, make no opposition to the establishment of posts and roads through their country, and allow travel free from their harassment. Hoffman also took some of their leading men or family members hostage. Afterward he left for San Bernardino, taking most of his force with him; others went down river by steamboat or overland to Fort Tejon.

Captain Armistead was left with two infantry companies and the column's artillery to garrison Hoffman's encampment at Beale's Crossing on the east bank of the Colorado River, Camp Colorado. Armistead renamed the post Fort Mojave. In late June 1859 the Mohave hostages escaped from Fort Yuma. Trouble broke out with the Mohave a few weeks later when they stole stock from a mail station that had been established two miles south of Fort Mojave, and attacked it. Mohaves tore up melons planted by the soldiers near the fort, and the soldiers shot a Mohave who was working in a garden. Eventually after a few weeks of aggressive patrolling and skirmishes, Armistead attacked the Mohave who returned fire in a battle between about 50 soldiers and 200 Mohave, resulting in three soldiers wounded. Twenty-three Mohave bodies were found but more were killed and wounded and removed by the Mohave. Following this defeat, the Mohave made a peace, which they kept from then on.[227]

Civil War

When the Civil War began, Captain Armistead was in command of the small garrison at the New San Diego Depot in San Diego, which was occupied in 1860. He was a close friend of Winfield Scott Hancock, serving with him as a quartermaster in Los Angeles, California, before the Civil War. Accounts say that in a farewell party before leaving to join the Confederate army, Armistead told Hancock, "Goodbye; you can never know what this has cost me."[228]

When the war started, Armistead departed from California to Texas with the Los Angeles Mounted Rifles, then traveled east and received a commission as a major, but was quickly promoted to colonel of the 57th Virginia Infantry regiment. He served in the western part of Virginia, but soon returned to the east and the Army of Northern Virginia. He fought as a brigade commander at Seven Pines, and then under General Robert E. Lee in the Seven Days Battles (where he was chosen to spearhead the bloody assault on Malvern Hill), and Second Bull Run. At Antietam, he served as Lee's provost marshal, a frustrating job due to the high levels of desertion that plagued the army in that

Figure 44: *This monument on the Gettysburg Battlefield marks the approximate place where Armistead was mortally wounded. The wall behind the monument marks the Union lines.*

campaign. Then he was under command in the division of Maj. Gen. George Pickett at Fredericksburg. Because he was with Lt. Gen. James Longstreet's First Corps near Norfolk, Virginia, in the spring of 1863, he missed the Battle of Chancellorsville.

In the Battle of Gettysburg, Armistead's brigade arrived the evening of July 2, 1863. Armistead was mortally wounded the next day while leading his brigade towards the center of the Union line in Pickett's Charge. Armistead led his brigade from the front, waving his hat from the tip of his saber, and reached the stone wall at the "Angle", which served as the charge's objective. The brigade got farther in the charge than any other, an event sometimes known as the High Water Mark of the Confederacy, but it was quickly overwhelmed by a Union counterattack. Armistead was shot three times just after crossing the wall. Union Captain Henry H. Bingham received Armistead's personal effects and carried the news to Union Major General Winfield Scott Hancock, who was Armistead's friend from before the war.[229]

Armistead's wounds were not believed to be mortal; he had been shot in the fleshy part of the arm and below the knee, and according to the surgeon who tended him, none of the wounds caused bone, artery, or nerve damage.[230] He was then taken to a Union field hospital at the George Spangler Farm[231] where he died two days later. Dr. Daniel Brinton, the chief surgeon at the Union hospital there, had expected Armistead to survive because he characterized the two bullet wounds as not of a "serious character." He wrote that the death "was not from his wounds directly, but from secondary bacterium, fever and prostration."[232]

Lewis Armistead is buried next to his uncle, Lieutenant Colonel George Armistead, commander of the garrison of Fort McHenry during the Battle of Baltimore, at the Old Saint Paul's Cemetery in Baltimore, Maryland.[233]

In popular media

In *Gettysburg*, the film version of Michael Shaara's novel *The Killer Angels*, Armistead was portrayed by actor Richard Jordan, who died shortly afterwards. In the film, the meeting between Armistead and Bingham at the High Water Mark was altered with Lt. Thomas Chamberlain (portrayed by C. Thomas Howell), brother of Col. Joshua Lawrence Chamberlain, taking Bingham's place. In the movie, Armistead was shot in the chest.

Actor John Prosky depicted Armistead for a special appearance in *Gods and Generals*, accompanying Pickett at Fredericksburg.

Armistead is a character in the alternate history novel *Gettysburg: A Novel of the Civil War* (2003) by Newt Gingrich and William Forstchen.

References

- Bessel, Paul M. "Masons." In *Encyclopedia of the American Civil War: A Political, Social, and Military History*, edited by David S. Heidler and Jeanne T. Heidler. New York: W. W. Norton & Company, 2000. <templatestyles src="Module:Citation/CS1/styles.css" />ISBN 0-393-04758-X.
- Eicher, John H., and David J. Eicher. *Civil War High Commands*. Stanford, CA: Stanford University Press, 2001. <templatestyles src="Module:Citation/CS1/styles.css" />ISBN 0-8047-3641-3.
- Foote, Shelby. *The Civil War: A Narrative*. Vol. 2, *Fredericksburg to Meridian*. New York: Random House, 1958. <templatestyles src="Module:Citation/CS1/styles.css" />ISBN 0-394-49517-9.
- Johnson, Charles Thomas. "Lewis Addison Armistead." In *Encyclopedia of the American Civil War: A Political, Social, and Military History*, edited by David S. Heidler and Jeanne T. Heidler. New York: W. W. Norton & Company, 2000. <templatestyles src="Module:Citation/CS1/styles.css" />ISBN 0-393-04758-X.

- Krick, Robert K. "Armistead and Garnett: The Parallel Lives of Two Virginia Soldiers." In *The Third Day at Gettysburg and Beyond*, edited by Gary W. Gallagher. Chapel Hill: University of North Carolina Press, 1998. <templatestyles src="Module:Citation/CS1/styles.css" />ISBN 0-8078-4753-4.
- Poindexter, Rev. James E. "General Armistead's Portrait Presented." *Southern Historical Society Papers* 37 (1909).
- Shaara, Michael. *The Killer Angels: A Novel*. New York: Ballantine Books, 2001. <templatestyles src="Module:Citation/CS1/styles.css" />ISBN 978-0-345-44412-7. First published 1974 by David McKay Co.
- Smith, Derek. *The Gallant Dead: Union & Confederate Generals Killed in the Civil War*. Mechanicsburg, PA: Stackpole Books, 2005. <templatestyles src="Module:Citation/CS1/styles.css" />ISBN 0-8117-0132-8.
- Tagg, Larry. *The Generals of Gettysburg*[234]. Campbell, CA: Savas Publishing, 1998. <templatestyles src="Module:Citation/CS1/styles.css" />ISBN 1-882810-30-9.
- Warner, Ezra J. *Generals in Gray: Lives of the Confederate Commanders*. Baton Rouge: Louisiana State University Press, 1959. <templatestyles src="Module:Citation/CS1/styles.css" />ISBN 0-8071-0823-5.
- Wert, Jeffry D. "Lewis Addison Armistead." In *The Confederate General*, vol. 1, edited by William C. Davis and Julie Hoffman. Harrisburg, PA: National Historical Society, 1991. <templatestyles src="Module:Citation/CS1/styles.css" />ISBN 0-918678-63-3.
- Wright, John D. *The Language of the Civil War*. Westport, CT: Oryx Press, 2001. <templatestyles src="Module:Citation/CS1/styles.css" />ISBN 978-1-57356-135-8.
- "Armistead's Death."[235] Gettysburg Discussion Group.

Further reading

- Motts, Wayne E. *Trust in God and Fear Nothing: Gen. Lewis A. Armistead, CSA*. Gettysburg, PA: Farnsworth House, 1994. <templatestyles src="Module:Citation/CS1/styles.css" />ISBN 978-0-9643632-0-5.

External links

- Lewis A. Armistead in *Encyclopedia Virginia*[236]
- Lewis Armistead[237] at Find a Grave
- *Confederate Veteran* article about Armistead from November 1914.[238] (This article is substantially the same text as Poindexter's *Southern Historical Society* paper.)

Elon J. Farnsworth

Elon John Farnsworth	
Born	July 30, 1837 Green Oak, Michigan
Died	July 3, 1863 (aged 25) Gettysburg, Pennsylvania
Place of burial	Rockton Cemetery, Rockton, Illinois
Allegiance	United States of America Union
Service/<wbr/>branch	United States Army Union Army
Years of service	1861–1863
Rank	Captain
Commands held	8th Illinois Cavalry Regiment 1st Brigade, 3rd Division, Cavalry Corps, Army of the Potomac
Battles/wars	Utah War American Civil War • Battle of Chancellorsville • Battle of Gettysburg †
Signature	

Elon John Farnsworth (July 30, 1837 – July 3, 1863) was a Union Army captain in the American Civil War. He commanded Brigade 1, Division 3 of the Cavalry Corps (Union Army) from June 28, 1863 to July 3, 1863, when he was mortally wounded and died at the Battle of Gettysburg. He was nominated by President Abraham Lincoln for appointment to the grade of brigadier general on June 29, 1863 but was not confirmed by the United States Senate before his death at Gettysburg.

Early life and career

Farnsworth was born in Green Oak, Michigan on July 30, 1837.[239]

Elon Farnsworth's uncle, John F. Farnsworth, served in the United States House of Representatives from Illinois between March 4, 1857 and March 3, 1861 and again between March 4, 1863 and March 3, 1873. John Farnsworth was a Union Army colonel who also commanded cavalry brigades (September 1862 to February 1862) and was nominated for appointed to the grade of brigadier general (November 1862). His appointment also was not confirmed by the United States Senate after the nomination was ordered returned to President Lincoln on February 12, 1863.

Elon Farnsworth's family moved to Illinois in 1854. A member of the Chi Psi Fraternity, Farnsworth was expelled from the University of Michigan following a drinking party in which a classmate died after being thrown from a window.[240] He joined the Army as a civilian foragemaster in 1857 and served on the staff of Albert Sidney Johnston during the Utah War of 1857–58.Wikipedia:Citation needed He also worked as a buffalo hunter, scout and freighter in the Colorado Territory.

Civil War

At the outbreak of the Civil War, Farnsworth was appointed a first lieutenant in the 8th Illinois Cavalry, the regiment commanded by his uncle, serving with distinction throughout the early stages of the war. Being promoted to captain on December 25, 1861, he was made Assistant Chief Quartermaster of the IV Corps, and in early 1863, he served as aide-de-camp to Brigadier General Alfred Pleasonton through the Battle of Chancellorsville and early stages of the Gettysburg Campaign. Pleasanton, then in command of the Union Cavalry Corp, gave Farnsworth command of 1st Brigade, 3rd Division, Cavalry Corps, Army of the Potomac on June 28, 1863, three days before the Battle of Gettysburg. On June 29, 1863, just two days before the battle, President Lincoln nominated Farnsworth to the grade brigadier general of volunteers but the appointment was never confirmed by the United States Senate.

Death at Gettysburg

After the collapse of Pickett's Charge and the defeat of Major General J.E.B. Stuart's Confederate cavalry on July 3, the third day of the Battle of Gettysburg, Brigadier General Hugh Judson Kilpatrick, commanding the 3rd Division, ordered Farnsworth to make a charge with his brigade against Confederate positions south of the Devil's Den area of the battlefield, below Little

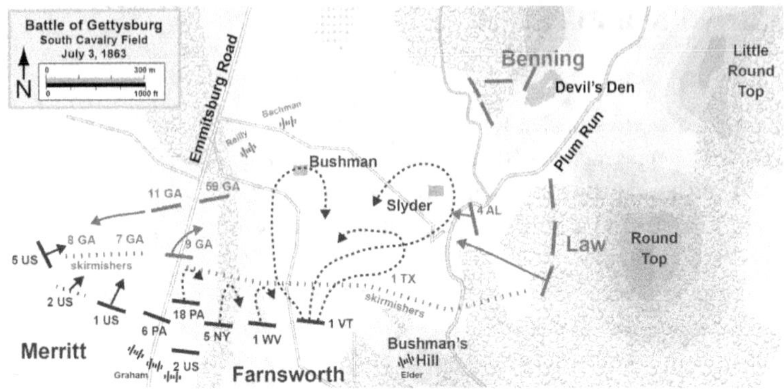

Figure 45:
South Cavalry Field at Gettysburg
Confederate
Union

Round Top. Farnsworth initially balked, arguing there was no hope of success, and only agreed to it when Kilpatrick allegedly accused him of cowardice. Farnsworth made the charge, against elements of John B. Hood's division, under Evander M. Law (Hood having been wounded the previous day). Farnsworth rode with the second battalion of the 1st Vermont Cavalry, alongside Major William Wells.

The charge was repulsed with heavy losses, and Farnsworth himself was shot five times in the chest. An account by Confederate Colonel William C. Oates claimed that Farnsworth was surrounded by Confederate soldiers and committed suicide to avoid capture, but this has been disputed by other witnesses and discounted by most historians.[241] Kilpatrick received much criticism for ordering the charge, but no official action was taken against him.

Farnsworth is buried in Rockton Cemetery, Rockton, Illinois.

Memorials

Battery Farnsworth, a coastal defense built between 1897 and 1899 near Fort Constitution at New Castle, New Hampshire, was named in his honor.

References

- Boatner, Mark Mayo, III. *The Civil War Dictionary*. New York: McKay, 1988. <templatestyles src="Module:Citation/CS1/styles.css" />ISBN 0-8129-1726-X. First published 1959 by McKay.
- Eicher, John H., and David J. Eicher. *Civil War High Commands*. Stanford, CA: Stanford University Press, 2001. <templatestyles src="Module:Citation/CS1/styles.css" />ISBN 0-8047-3641-3.
- Symonds, Craig L. *American Heritage History of the Battle of Gettysburg*. New York: HarperCollins, 2001. <templatestyles src="Module:Citation/CS1/styles.css" />ISBN 0-06-019474-X.
- Wert, Jeffry D. *Gettysburg: Day Three*. New York: Simon & Schuster, 2001. <templatestyles src="Module:Citation/CS1/styles.css" />ISBN 0-684-85914-9.

External links

- "Elon J. Farnsworth"[242]. Find a Grave. Retrieved August 15, 2010.<templatestyles src="Module:Citation/CS1/styles.css"></templatestyles>
- "Farnsworth, John Franklin" [243]. *Appletons' Cyclopædia of American Biography*. 1900.<templatestyles src="Module:Citation/CS1/styles.css"></templatestyles>

Richard B. Garnett

Richard Brooke Garnett	
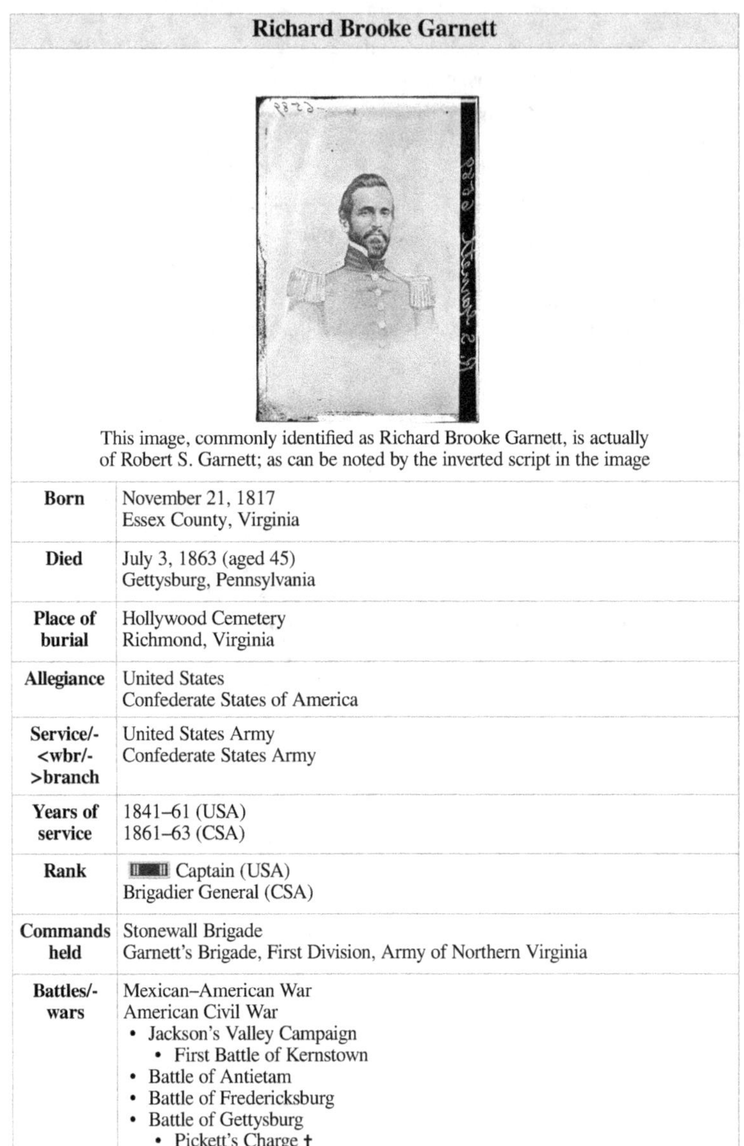 This image, commonly identified as Richard Brooke Garnett, is actually of Robert S. Garnett; as can be noted by the inverted script in the image	
Born	November 21, 1817 Essex County, Virginia
Died	July 3, 1863 (aged 45) Gettysburg, Pennsylvania
Place of burial	Hollywood Cemetery Richmond, Virginia
Allegiance	United States Confederate States of America
Service/-<wbr/->branch	United States Army Confederate States Army
Years of service	1841–61 (USA) 1861–63 (CSA)
Rank	Captain (USA) Brigadier General (CSA)
Commands held	Stonewall Brigade Garnett's Brigade, First Division, Army of Northern Virginia

Battles/-wars	Mexican–American War
	American Civil War
	• Jackson's Valley Campaign
	  • First Battle of Kernstown
	• Battle of Antietam
	• Battle of Fredericksburg
	• Battle of Gettysburg
	  • Pickett's Charge †

Richard Brooke Garnett (November 21, 1817 – July 3, 1863) was a career United States Army officer and a Confederate general in the American Civil War. He was court-martialed by Stonewall Jackson for his actions in command

of the Stonewall Brigade at the First Battle of Kernstown, and killed during
Pickett's Charge at the Battle of Gettysburg.

Early life

Garnett was born on the "Rose Hill" estate in Essex County, Virginia, the son
of William Henry Garnett and Anna Maria Brooke, both of primarily English
ancestry. He had a twin brother, William, who died in Norfolk in 1855. He
was the cousin of Robert M. T. Hunter as well as Robert Selden Garnett, also a
Confederate general, who holds the dubious distinction of being the first general officer killed during the Civil War. Both of the Garnetts graduated from
the United States Military Academy in 1841, with Richard standing 29th out
of 52 cadets, two spots below Robert.[244] Garnett was commissioned as a second lieutenant in the 6th U.S. Infantry and he served in a variety of posts in
Florida, fighting the Seminoles, and then in the West, where he commanded
Fort Laramie, rode with the Utah Expedition, and was a noted Indian fighter.

During the Mexican–American War, he served in staff positions in New Orleans, and was promoted to first lieutenant on February 16, 1847. He learned of
the outbreak of the Civil War while serving in California as a captain, the rank
to which he had been promoted on May 9, 1855. Despite believing strongly
that the Union should not be dissolved, he returned to Virginia to fight for his
native state and the Confederacy.

Civil War

Garnett resigned his commission in the U.S. Army on May 17, 1861, and
entered the Confederate States Army. His first assignment in Virginia was as
a major of artillery in May, and then as lieutenant colonel of Cobb's Georgia
Legion on August 31. He was promoted to brigadier general on November 14,
1861, and commanded the 1st Brigade of the Valley District of the Confederate
Army of the Potomac, which was the brigade originally formed by Thomas
J. "Stonewall" Jackson, the Stonewall Brigade; Jackson was now in overall
command in the Shenandoah Valley.

During Jackson's Valley Campaign of 1862, Garnett's military career took a
downward turn at the First Battle of Kernstown in March. Jackson marched his
army 40 miles (64 km) to intercept a portion of the Union Army under Maj.
Gen. Nathaniel P. Banks. On March 23, Jackson's cavalry commander, Col.
Turner Ashby, brought faulty intelligence that the retreating Union division of
Brig. Gen. James Shields had four regiments in the rear outside Winchester,
Virginia. Since that force was of comparable size to Jackson's, he ordered
Garnett and the Stonewall Brigade to attack. Unfortunately, Shields had a full

infantry division on hand, almost 9,000 men, twice the size of Jackson's force. The attack went badly and Garnett, finding his brigade low on ammunition and surrounded by forces attacking from three sides, ordered a retreat. Jackson was infuriated and accused Garnett of disobeying orders, meaning that he should not have retreated without obtaining permission from Jackson first. Jackson, well known as a strict disciplinarian, arrested Garnett for "neglect of duty" on April 1 and relieved him of command. Garnett's court-martial started in August 1862, with only Jackson and his aide giving testimony. However the trial was suspended due to the start of Gen. Robert E. Lee's Northern Virginia Campaign and the Second Battle of Bull Run that August.

Lee ordered Jackson to release Garnett from arrest and he was assigned to command the injured George Pickett's brigade in Lt. Gen. James Longstreet's First Corps in the Army of Northern Virginia. Garnett commanded the brigade credibly at the Battle of Antietam in September, after which he assumed permanent command of the brigade on November 26 when Pickett was promoted to divisional command, and at the Battle of Fredericksburg that December. He did not participate in the Battle of Chancellorsville in May 1863 because Longstreet's Corps was assigned duties in Suffolk, Virginia.

Stonewall Jackson was gravely wounded at Chancellorsville and died soon after from pneumonia. Upon Jackson's death, Garnett returned to Richmond where the general's body lay in state. Despite his professional disagreement with Jackson, Garnett set aside any ill will against him and served as a pall bearer[245] along with Longstreet, Richard S. Ewell, and others at his funeral.

Gettysburg and death

During the Gettysburg Campaign, Garnett's brigade continued in the division of George Pickett and, due to the order of march, did not reach the battlefield from Chambersburg, Pennsylvania, until late on the afternoon of July 2, 1863, missing the first two days of the Battle of Gettysburg. Pickett's division was assigned by Gen. Lee to lead a great assault on the Union's center on Cemetery Ridge on July 3. Garnett's brigade was in the front rank of Pickett's division, on the left, next to Brig. Gen. James L. Kemper's brigade. Garnett was in no shape to lead an infantry charge; he was suffering from fever and an injured leg when his horse kicked him and could not walk. But Garnett yearned to settle the record of his military dishonor from Kernstown, which the aborted court-martial could not. Despite protestations from other officers, Garnett insisted on leading his soldiers into battle on horseback, becoming a conspicuous target for Union riflemen.Wikipedia:Citation needed

Prior to starting out toward the Union defenses on Cemetery Hill, Garnett conversed with Brig. Gen. Lewis Armistead, another of Pickett's brigade

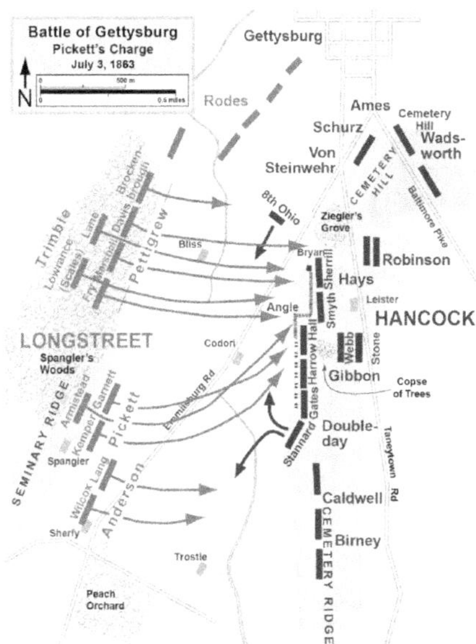

Figure 46:
Map of Pickett's Charge, July 3, 1863.
Confederate
Union

commanders, about the proposed charge. Garnett reportedly said: "This is a desperate thing to attempt." to which Armistead added his prediction that "the slaughter will be terrible."[246]

Garnett got within 20 yards of the "Angle" on Cemetery Ridge before he was killed, a bullet striking him in the head as he waved his hat to urge his men forward.[247,248] His courier, Private Robert H. Irvine of the 19th Virginia, witnessed his death. Irvine's horse was hit and fell on Garnett, so the private pulled Garnett's body from underneath the animal and retrieved the general's watch, which he gave to the brigade adjutant. There are conflicting stories about whether Garnett's horse, a bay gelding named Red Eye, returned to the Confederate lines.[249] Although Garnett was wearing a new uniform,[250] somehow his body was never identified and he was buried by Union soldiers in a mass grave. Robert K. Krick presumes that his remains were later transferred to Hollywood Cemetery in Richmond.[251] Garnett, Armistead, and Kemper were three of the 17 Confederate general-officer casualties during the three-day battle.[252]

In memoriam

In 1872, remains of Confederate dead were brought from Gettysburg and rein-
terred to Hollywood Cemetery in Richmond, Virginia. The Hollywood Memorial Association erected a cenotaph in Garnett's honor in 1991, making the
assumption that his remains were in this group. Years after the war, Garnett's
sword was located in a Baltimore pawnshop and was purchased by former
Confederate Brig. Gen. George H. Steuart, who died before he could return
it to Garnett's family. It was subsequently returned by Steuart's nephew.[253]

In popular media

Garnett was portrayed by American actor Andrew Prine in the 1993 film *Gettysburg*, based on Michael Shaara's novel, *The Killer Angels*. In the movie,
Garnett is killed by a cannon shot and his horse returns to the southern lines
riderless, perhaps to reflect how his body was never found. He reprised this
role in 2003 in film's prequel *Gods and Generals*, although uncredited and
without any dialog.

Disputed photograph

The photograph of Richard Garnett in this article is one of only two known
and it may in fact be of his cousin Robert S. Garnett instead.[254] A letter to the
editor of *America's Civil War* magazine claims that the Library of Congress
possesses a photograph of Richard B. Garnett that has been mislabeled as
"Franklin Gardner, CSA, Born N.Y.C."[255]

References

- Eicher, John H., and David J. Eicher, *Civil War High Commands*. Stanford: Stanford University Press, 2001. <templatestyles
  src="Module:Citation/CS1/styles.css" />ISBN 978-0-8047-3641-1.
- Hess, Earl J. *Pickett's Charge—The Last Attack at Gettysburg*. Chapel
  Hill: University of North Carolina Press, 2001. <templatestyles
  src="Module:Citation/CS1/styles.css" />ISBN 0-8078-2648-0.
- Krick, Robert K. "Armistead and Garnett: The Parallel Lives of Two
  Virginia Soldiers." In *The Third Day at Gettysburg & Beyond*, edited
  by Gary W. Gallagher. Chapel Hill: University of North Carolina Press,
  1994. <templatestyles src="Module:Citation/CS1/styles.css" />ISBN 0-
  8078-4753-4.

Figure 47: *Library of Congress photograph labeled "Franklin Gard-ner, CSA, Born N.Y.C.," which may actually be Richard B. Garnett*

Figure 48: *"Franklin Gardner" picture.*

- Sifakis, Stewart. *Who Was Who in the Civil War*. New York: Facts On File, 1988. <templatestyles src="Module:Citation/CS1/styles.css" />ISBN 978-0-8160-1055-4.
- Tagg, Larry. *The Generals of Gettysburg*[256]. Campbell, CA: Savas Publishing, 1998. <templatestyles src="Module:Citation/CS1/styles.css" />ISBN 1-882810-30-9.
- Warner, Ezra J. *Generals in Gray: Lives of the Confederate Commanders*. Baton Rouge: Louisiana State University Press, 1959. <templatestyles src="Module:Citation/CS1/styles.css" />ISBN 978-0-8071-0823-9.
- Wert, Jeffry D. *General James Longstreet: The Confederacy's Most Controversial Soldier: A Biography*. New York: Simon & Schuster, 1993. <templatestyles src="Module:Citation/CS1/styles.css" />ISBN 0-671-70921-6.

External links

Wikisourcehas the text of a 1900 *Appletons' Cyclopædia of American Biography*article about **Richard B. Garnett**.

- Richard B. Garnett in *Encyclopedia Virginia*[257]
- Online biography[258]

Retreat from Gettysburg

J. Johnston Pettigrew

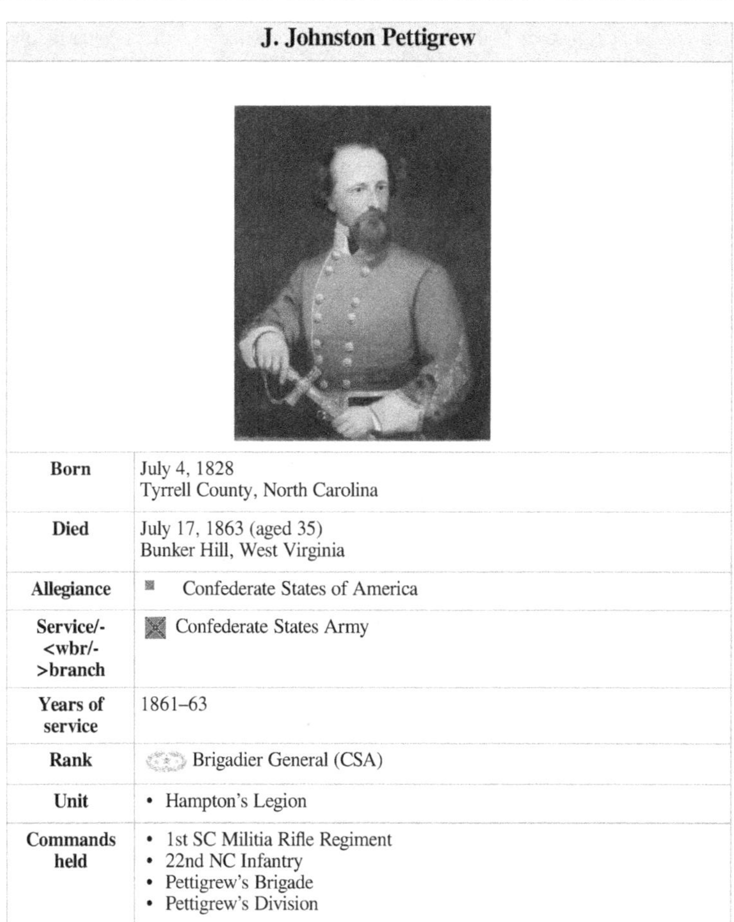

J. Johnston Pettigrew	
Born	July 4, 1828 Tyrrell County, North Carolina
Died	July 17, 1863 (aged 35) Bunker Hill, West Virginia
Allegiance	Confederate States of America
Service/<wbr/>branch	Confederate States Army
Years of service	1861–63
Rank	Brigadier General (CSA)
Unit	• Hampton's Legion
Commands held	• 1st SC Militia Rifle Regiment • 22nd NC Infantry • Pettigrew's Brigade • Pettigrew's Division

Battles/wars	American Civil War • Battle of Gettysburg

James Johnston Pettigrew (July 4, 1828 – July 17, 1863) was an author, lawyer, linguist, diplomat, and soldier. As a Confederate general in the American Civil War, he was one of three division commanders in the disastrous assault known as Pickett's Charge on the final day of the Battle of Gettysburg. He was badly wounded during the assault and killed by a Union attack during the Confederate retreat to Virginia.Wikipedia:Citation needed

Early years

Johnston Pettigrew was born to Ebenezer and Ann Sheppard Pettigrew in Tyrrell County, North Carolina. His father was of a wealthy family of French Huguenot background.[259] His mother and the mother of Union general John Gibbon were first cousins, making Gibbon and Pettigrew second cousins. Pettigrew entered the University of North Carolina at Chapel Hill at the age of 15. He excelled in mathematics and classical languages, and was a member of the Philanthropic Society. He also led his class in fencing and boxing. He earned praise for his achievements from President James K. Polk, who appointed him an assistant professor at the United States Naval Observatory. He then studied law in Baltimore and joined the firm of his father's first cousin, James Louis Petigru in Charleston, South Carolina, followed by a trip to Germany to study civil law. He traveled around Europe for seven years, where he learned to speak and write French, Spanish, German, and Italian, and to read Greek, Hebrew, and Arabic. He wrote a travel book, *Notes on Spain and the Spaniards*, and spent time in the diplomatic service.Wikipedia:Citation needed

Returning to the U.S., Pettigrew was elected to the South Carolina legislature in 1856. Despite his gift of foreign languages and civil knowledge, Pettigrew leaned toward the military as a way to serve his country and his state. In December 1860, he was serving as an aide to the governor of South Carolina and the following April participated in the negotiations between the governor's office, South Carolina military authorities, and the Union commander of Fort Sumter in Charleston Harbor.Wikipedia:Citation needed

Civil War

When war began, Pettigrew joined the Hampton Legion, a force raised in South Carolina by Wade Hampton, as a private, although he quickly accepted a commission as colonel of the 1st South Carolina Rifle Militia Regiment. He returned to North Carolina to command the 12th (later renamed the 22nd)

Figure 49: *Pettigrew circa 1855.*

North Carolina Infantry. Both Jefferson Davis and Gen. Joseph E. Johnston urged him to accept higher command, but he declined because of his lack of military experience. However, as the need for qualified officers in the Confederate States Army became acute, the new colonel was soon ordered to Virginia to accept a promotion to brigadier general on February 26, 1862.Wikipedia:Citation needed

When a young relative requested a "safe place" on Pettigrew's staff, he replied: "I assure you that the most unsafe place in the Brigade is about me. By all means let him get rid of this idea of a safe place, which he will regret after time. The post of danger is certainly the post of honor." He was true to his word.Wikipedia:Citation needed

Peninsula Campaign

During the Peninsula Campaign in the summer of 1862, Pettigrew was severely wounded at the Battle of Seven Pines. He was hit by a Minié ball that damaged his throat, windpipe, and shoulder. Pettigrew nearly bled to death, and while lying wounded, he received another bullet wound in the arm and was bayoneted in the right leg. Believing his wounds mortal, Pettigrew did not permit any of his men to leave the ranks to carry him to the rear. Left for dead on the field, he recovered consciousness as a Union prisoner of war.[260] Exchanged two months

Figure 50: *Edgewood Manor home.*

later, the general recovered from his wounds, spent the fall commanding a brigade in Maj. Gen. Daniel Harvey Hill's division around Richmond, and in the winter commanded a brigade in North Carolina and southern Virginia. He returned to his North Carolina brigade just in time to begin the Gettysburg Campaign in June 1863.Wikipedia:Citation needed

Gettysburg Campaign

The Confederate War Department had assigned Pettigrew's Brigade to Gen. Robert E. Lee's Army of Northern Virginia, and Pettigrew traveled to Fredericksburg, Virginia, to rejoin that army in late May. Pettigrew's Brigade was the strongest in Maj. Gen. Henry Heth's Division of Lt. Gen. A.P. Hill's Third Corps. Freshly uniformed and armed with rifles from state military depots, his regiments presented a fine military appearance during the march through Maryland and Pennsylvania. Some of his regimental officers were also members of the North Carolina planter "aristocracy", including Colonel Collett Leventhorpe leading the 11th North Carolina Infantry and twenty-one-year-old Harry Burgwyn at the head of the 26th North Carolina Regiment, the largest Confederate regiment at Gettysburg. Not having been in serious combat for nearly a year, his brigade mustered a strength over 2,500 officers and men.[261]

Figure 51: *Monument*

Figure 52: *Bronze Plaque.*

Pettigrew's Brigade tangled with the Iron Brigade on July 1, 1863, at the McPherson and Herbst farms to the west of Gettysburg, where all four of his regiments suffered devastating losses—over 40 percent—but were successful in driving the Union forces off of McPherson's Ridge. General Pettigrew assumed command of the division after the wounding of Gen. Heth that afternoon, and attempted to reorganize the battered division during the next day's battle as they lay behind Seminary Ridge.Wikipedia:Citation needed

On July 3, 1863, Gen. Lee selected Pettigrew's division to march at the left of Maj. Gen. George Pickett's in the famous infantry assault popularly known as Pickett's Charge (sometimes called "Longstreet's Assault" or the "Pickett-Pettigrew-Trimble Assault", since Pickett led only one third of the men engaged in the attack). Lee had not consulted with Pettigrew beforehand and was unaware of the terrible condition of Pettigrew's division.Wikipedia:Citation needed

As the division advanced, it received murderous fire. After Pettigrew's horse was shot out from under him, he continued on foot. As he approached within 100 yards (90 meters) of the stone wall on Cemetery Ridge (which was partially held by his cousin John Gibbon, leading Second Division of the Union II Corps), he was severely wounded in the left hand by canister fire. Despite being in great pain, Pettigrew remained with his soldiers until it was obvious that the attack had failed. Holding his bloody hand, as Pettigrew was retreating towards Seminary Ridge, he encountered General Lee. Pettigrew attempted to speak, but Lee, seeing the wound, spoke first: "General, I am sorry to see you are wounded; go to the rear." With a painful salute, Pettigrew continued to the rear.Wikipedia:Citation needed

During the Confederate retreat from Gettysburg, Pettigrew remained in command until Heth recovered. Stopped by the flooded Potomac River at Falling Waters, West Virginia, Pettigrew's brigade was deployed in a dense skirmish line on the Maryland side, in order to protect the road to the river crossing. Union cavalry probed the southern defenses throughout the night as Lee's army crossed the pontoon bridges into West Virginia. On the morning of July 14, 1863, Pettigrew's brigade was one of the last Confederate units still north of the Potomac River when the Union attacked his position. On foot and in the front line, Pettigrew was directing his soldiers when he was shot by a Union cavalryman from the Michigan Brigade at close range, the bullet striking him in the abdomen. He was immediately carried to the rear and across the Potomac, having refused to be left in federal hands. He died three days later at Edgewood Manor plantation near Bunker Hill, West Virginia. His brigade, which lost an estimated 56% casualties, had been ruined as an effective combat organization.[262]

Figure 53: *Tyrrell County Confederate Monument noting the death of General J. Johnston Pettigrew, located on the court-house lawn, East Main Street in Columbia, North Carolina.*

Legacy

The loss of Pettigrew emotionally devastated his family. An official day of mourning was held for him in North Carolina. His death also affected Lee, who remarked: "The army has lost a brave soldier and the Confederacy an accomplished officer."[263] General Pettigrew's body was returned to North Carolina and interred at his family estate, "Bonarva", which is now part of Pettigrew State Park in Washington and Tyrrell Counties.Wikipedia:Citation needed

General James Johnston Pettigrew Camp #1401 of the Sons of Confederate Veterans in Lenoir, North Carolina, was named for the fallen officer.Wikipedia:Citation needed

In World War II, the United States liberty ship SS *James J. Pettigrew* was named in his honor.

In popular media

Pettigrew was portrayed by actor George Lazenby in the definitive film *Gettysburg* (1993). At the time of filming, Lazenby was approximately 53, an age the real Pettigrew never reached.Wikipedia:Citation needed

Mackinlay Kantor's alternate history novella *If the South Had Won the Civil War* quotes passages from a chronicle of the CSA's early years of independence, written by a longer-lived Pettigrew.Wikipedia:Citation needed

Bibliography

- Busey, John W., and David G. Martin. *Regimental Strengths and Losses at Gettysburg*. 4th ed. Hightstown, NJ: Longstreet House, 2005. <templatestyles src="Module:Citation/CS1/styles.css" />ISBN 0-944413-67-6.
- Eicher, John H., and David J. Eicher, *Civil War High Commands*. Stanford: Stanford University Press, 2001. <templatestyles src="Module:Citation/CS1/styles.css" />ISBN 978-0-8047-3641-1.
- Gottfried, Bradley M. *Brigades of Gettysburg*. New York: Da Capo Press, 2002. <templatestyles src="Module:Citation/CS1/styles.css" />ISBN 0-306-81175-8.
- Hess, Earl J. *Lee's Tar Heels: The Pettigrew-Kirkland-MacRae Brigade*. Chapel Hill: University of North Carolina Press, 2002. <templatestyles src="Module:Citation/CS1/styles.css" />ISBN 0-8078-2687-1.
- Sifakis, Stewart. *Who Was Who in the Civil War*. New York: Facts On File, 1988. <templatestyles src="Module:Citation/CS1/styles.css" />ISBN 978-0-8160-1055-4.
- Tagg, Larry. *The Generals of Gettysburg*[264]. Campbell, CA: Savas Publishing, 1998. <templatestyles src="Module:Citation/CS1/styles.css" />ISBN 1-882810-30-9.
- U.S. War Department. *The War of the Rebellion*[265]: *a Compilation of the Official Records of the Union and Confederate Armies*. Washington, DC: U.S. Government Printing Office, 1880–1901.
- Warner, Ezra J. *Generals in Gray: Lives of the Confederate Commanders*. Baton Rouge: Louisiana State University Press, 1959. <templatestyles src="Module:Citation/CS1/styles.css" />ISBN 978-0-8071-0823-9.

Further reading

- Wilson, Clyde N. *Carolina Cavalier: The Life and Mind of James Johnston Pettigrew*. Athens: University of Georgia Press, 1990. <templatestyles src="Module:Citation/CS1/styles.css" />ISBN 978-0-8203-1201-9.

- Gragg, Rod. *Covered With Glory: The 26th North Carolina Infantry at Gettysburg*. New York: HarperCollins, 2000. <templatestyles src="Module:Citation/CS1/styles.css" />ISBN 978-0-06-017445-3.
- Stewart, George R. (1959). *Pickett's Charge: A Microhistory of the Final Attack at Gettysburg, July 3, 1863*. Boston: Houghton Mifflin. LCCN 59-8864[266].<templatestyles src="Module:Citation/CS1/styles.css"></templatestyles>
- Trescot, William Henry. *Memorial of the Life of J. Johnston Pettigrew: Brigadier General of the Confederate States Army*[267]. Charleston, SC: J. Russell, 1870. <templatestyles src="Module:Citation/CS1/styles.css" />OCLC 3557938[268].

External links

- "J. Johnston Pettigrew"[269]. Find a Grave. Retrieved 2008-06-27.<templatestyles src="Module:Citation/CS1/styles.css"></templatestyles>
- National Park Service biography[270]
- Pettigrew State Park[271]
- Photos of Pettigrew[272] at the Wayback Machine (archived February 8, 2008)
- Confederate memorial addresses : Monday, May 11, 1885, New Bern, N. C (1886)- includes biographical sketch of James Johnston Pettigrew[273]

Deathbed promotion

Strong Vincent

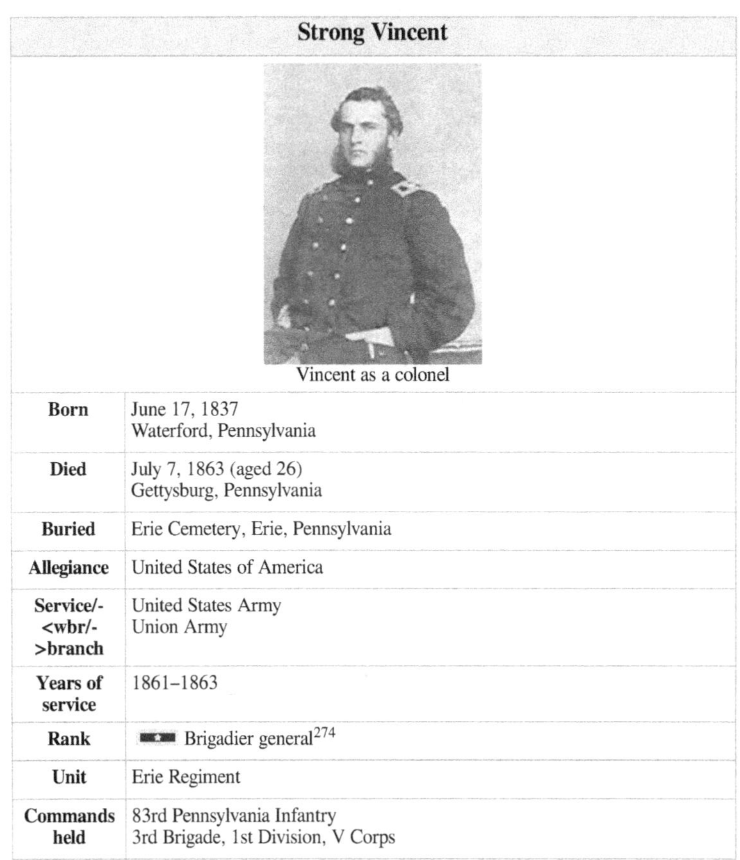
Vincent as a colonel

	Strong Vincent
Born	June 17, 1837 Waterford, Pennsylvania
Died	July 7, 1863 (aged 26) Gettysburg, Pennsylvania
Buried	Erie Cemetery, Erie, Pennsylvania
Allegiance	United States of America
Service/<wbr/>branch	United States Army Union Army
Years of service	1861–1863
Rank	Brigadier general[274]
Unit	Erie Regiment
Commands held	83rd Pennsylvania Infantry 3rd Brigade, 1st Division, V Corps

Battles/wars	• American Civil War Battle of Gaines's Mill Battle of Fredericksburg Battle of Gettysburg (<u>DOW</u>)

Strong Vincent (June 17, 1837 – July 7, 1863) was a lawyer who became famous as a U.S. Army officer during the American Civil War. He was mortally wounded while leading his brigade during the fighting at Little Round Top on the second day of the Battle of Gettysburg, and died five days later.

Early life and education

Vincent was born in Waterford, Pennsylvania, son of iron foundryman B. B. Vincent and Sarah Ann (née) Strong. He attended Trinity College and Harvard University, graduating in 1859. He practiced law in Erie, Pennsylvania.

American Civil War

At the start of the American Civil War, Vincent joined the Pennsylvania Militia as an adjutant and first lieutenant of the Erie Regiment. On September 14, 1861, he was commissioned lieutenant colonel of the 83rd Pennsylvania Infantry and was promoted to colonel the following June. After the death of his regimental commander in the Seven Days Battles (at the Battle of Gaines's Mill), Vincent assumed command of the regiment. He developed malaria on the Virginia Peninsula and was on medical leave until the Battle of Fredericksburg in December 1862. On May 20, 1863, he assumed command of the 3rd Brigade, 1st Division, V Corps, Army of the Potomac, replacing his brigade commander, who resigned after the Battle of Chancellorsville.

At the Battle of Gettysburg, 26-year-old Vincent and his brigade arrived on July 2, 1863. He had started the Gettysburg Campaign knowing that his young wife, Elizabeth H. Carter, whom he had married on the day he enlisted in the army, was pregnant with their first child. He had written her, "If I fall, remember you have given your husband to the most righteous cause that ever widowed a woman."

Maj. Gen. Daniel E. Sickles of the III Corps had deviated from his orders, moving his corps to a position that left undefended a significant terrain feature: Little Round Top. The chief engineer of the Army of the Potomac, Brig. Gen. Gouverneur K. Warren, recognized the tactical importance of the hill and urgently sought Union troops to occupy it before the Confederates could. A staff officer sent by Warren encountered Vincent's brigade nearby. Vincent, without consulting his superior officers, decided that his brigade was in the

Figure 54: *Likeness of Col. Vincent atop the 83rd Pennsylvania Infantry monument, Gettysburg National Military Park near the spot where Vincent was mortally wounded*

ideal position to defend Little Round Top, saying "I will take the responsibility to take my brigade there." Pvt. Oliver Willcox Norton, Vincent's brigade standard bearer and bugler, later wrote that he and Vincent made a reconnaissance of the Confederate forces as the brigade was moving into position, "While our line was forming on the hill at Gettysburg I came out with him in full view of the rebel lines. They opened two batteries on us instantly, firing at the colors. Colonel Vincent looked to see what was drawing the fire and yelled at me, "Down with the flag, Norton! Damn it, go behind the rocks with it.".[275]

One of Vincent's regiments, the 20th Maine, led by Colonel Joshua Lawrence Chamberlain, has received most of the fame for the defense of Little Round Top, but there is little doubt that the efforts and bravery of Vincent were instrumental in the eventual Union victory. Vincent impressed upon Chamberlain the importance of his position on the brigade's left flank and then he left to attend to the brigade's right flank. There, the 16th Michigan Infantry was starting to yield to enemy pressure. Mounting a large boulder, Vincent brandished a riding crop given to him by his wife and shouted to his men "Don't give an inch!" A bullet struck him through the thigh and the groin and he fell. Due to the determination of the 20th Maine, the 44th New York, the 83rd Pennsylvania and the 16th Michigan Infantry, the Union line held against the

Figure 55: *The pennant of the 3rd Brigade*

Confederate onslaught. Vincent was carried from the hill to a nearby farm, where he lay dying for the next five days, unable to be transported home due to the severity of his injury.

The commander of the Army of the Potomac, Maj. Gen. George G. Meade, recommended Vincent for promotion to brigadier general on the evening of July 2. The promotion was dated July 3, 1863, but it is doubtful that Vincent knew about the honor before he died[276] (although Pvt. Oliver Willcox Norton in *Army Letters 1861-1865* writes "His commission as Brigadier General was read to him on his deathbed.")[277] Vincent's wife gave birth to a baby girl two months later, who died before reaching the age of one and is buried next to her father.

His corps commander, Maj. Gen. George Sykes, described Vincent's actions in his official report from the battle:

<templatestyles src="Template:Quote/styles.css"/>

Night closed the fight. The key of the battle-field was in our possession intact. Vincent, Weed, and Hazlett, chiefs lamented throughout the corps and army, sealed with their lives the spot intrusted to their keeping, and on which so much depended.... General Weed and Colonel Vincent, officers of rare promise, gave their lives to their country.

—George Sykes, report on the Battle of Gettysburg

Figure 56: *Statue at Blasco Library in Erie, Pennsylvania*

Legacy

Vincent is buried in Erie Cemetery in Erie. He is memorialized by a statue on the 83rd Pennsylvania monument on Little Round Top, by a statue erected in 1997 at Blasco Memorial Library, Erie, and by Strong Vincent High School (now a middle school) in Erie. The portion of Little Round Top to the southeast of Sykes Avenue on the Gettysburg Battlefield is known as "Vincent's Spur". The 1-112 Infantry of the Pennsylvania Army National Guard stationed in Cambridge Springs uses the call sign "STRONG" in recognition of Vincent's courage, determination and sacrifice.

In popular culture

- Vincent is a character in the novel *The Killer Angels* by Michael Shaara. In its 1993 film adaptation *Gettysburg*, he is portrayed by Maxwell Caulfield.
- Vincent is a character in the alternate history novel "Gettysburg: A Novel of the Civil War" by Newt Gingrich and William R. Forstchen.

References

- Eicher, John H., and David J. Eicher. *Civil War High Commands*. Stanford, CA: Stanford University Press, 2001. <templatestyles src="Module:Citation/CS1/styles.css" />ISBN 0-8047-3641-3.
- Goellnitz, Jenny. Online biography of Vincent[278].
- Norton, Oliver W. *Army Letters 1861-1865*[279]. Dayton, OH: Morningside, 1990. <templatestyles src="Module:Citation/CS1/styles.css" />OCLC 24611059[280].
- Warner, Ezra J. *Generals in Blue: Lives of the Union Commanders*. Baton Rouge: Louisiana State University Press, 1964. <templatestyles src="Module:Citation/CS1/styles.css" />ISBN 0-8071-0822-7.

Further reading

- Norton, Oliver W. *The Attack and Defense of Little Round Top: Gettysburg, July 2, 1863*[281]. Gettysburg, PA: Stan Clark Military Books, 1992. <templatestyles src="Module:Citation/CS1/styles.css" />ISBN 1-879664-08-9. First published 1913 by Stan Clark/Neale.

Appendix

References

[1] //tools.wmflabs.org/geohack/geohack.php?pagename=Battle_of_Gettysburg¶ms=39.
811_N_77.225_W_type:event_region:US_scale:30000

[2] Coddington, p. 573. See the discussion regarding historians' judgment on whether Gettysburg should be considered a decisive victory.

[3] *Official Records*, Series I, Volume XXVII, Part 1, pages 155–168 http://ebooks.library.cornell.
edu/cgi/t/text/pageviewer-idx?c=moawar&cc=moawar&idno=waro0043&node=waro0043%
3A2&view=image&seq=175&size=100

[4] *Official Records*, Series I, Volume XXVII, Part 2, pages 283–291 http://ebooks.library.cornell.
edu/cgi/t/text/pageviewer-idx?c=moawar&cc=moawar&idno=waro0044&node=waro0044%
3A2&view=image&seq=285&size=100

[5] *Official Records*, Series I, Volume XXVII, Part 1, page 151 http://ebooks.library.cornell.
edu/cgi/t/text/pageviewer-idx?c=moawar&cc=moawar&idno=waro0043&q1=return+of+
casualties&view=image&seq=193&size=100

[6] Busey and Martin, p. 125: "Engaged strength" at the battle was 93,921.

[7] Busey and Martin, p. 260, state that "engaged strength" at the battle was 71,699; McPherson, p. 648, lists the strength at the start of the campaign as 75,000.

[8] *Official Records*, Series I, Volume XXVII, Part 1, page 187 http://ebooks.library.cornell.
edu/cgi/t/text/pageviewer-idx?c=moawar&cc=moawar&idno=waro0043&q1=return+of+
casualties&view=image&seq=207&size=100

[9] Busey and Martin, p. 125.

[10] Busey and Martin, p. 260, cite **23,231** total (4,708 killed;12,693 wounded;5,830 captured/-missing).
See the section on casualties for a discussion of alternative Confederate casualty estimates, which have been cited as high as **28,000**.

[11] *Official Records*, Series I, Volume XXVII, Part 2, pages 338–346 http//ebooks.library.cornell.edu

[12] Robert D. Quigley, *Civil War Spoken Here: A Dictionary of Mispronounced People, Places and Things of the 1860's* (Collingswood, NJ: C. W. Historicals, 1993), p. 68.

[13] The Battle of Antietam, the culmination of Lee's first invasion of the North, had the largest number of casualties in a single day, about 23,000.

[14] Rawley, p. 147; Sauers, p. 827; Gallagher, *Lee and His Army*, p. 83; McPherson, p. 665; Eicher, p. 550. Gallagher and McPherson cite the combination of Gettysburg and Vicksburg as the turning point. Eicher uses the arguably related expression, "High-water mark of the Confederacy".

[15] Symonds, pp. 49–54.

[16] Coddington, pp. 8–9; Eicher, p. 490.

[17] Eicher, pp. 489–491.

[18] Symonds, p. 36.

[19] Trudeau, pp. 45, 66.

[20] Nye, pp. 272–278.

[21] Symonds, pp. 41–43; Sears, pp. 103–106; Esposito, text for Map 94 (Map 34b https://archive.
fo/20100607100747/http://www.military.com/Resources/ResourceFileView/civilwar_maps_
map34_largerview.htm in the online version); Eicher, pp. 504–507; McPherson, p. 649.

[22] Sears, p. 123; Trudeau, p. 128.

[23] Coddington, pp. 181, 189.

[24] Eicher, pp. 508–509, discounts Heth's claim because the previous visit by Early to Gettysburg would have made the lack of shoe factories or stores obvious. However, many mainstream historians accept Heth's account: Sears, p. 136; Foote, p. 465; Clark, p. 35; Tucker, pp. 97–98; Martin, p. 25; Pfanz, *First Day*, p. 25.

[25] Eicher, p. 508; Tucker, pp. 99–102.

[26] Eicher, pp. 502–503.

[27] Coddington, p. 122.

[28] Eicher, p. 503.

[29] Sears, pp. 155–158.

[30] Martin, pp. 80–81. The troopers carried single-shot, breechloading carbines manufactured by Sharps, Burnside, and others. It is a modern myth that they were armed with multi-shot repeating carbines. Nevertheless, they were able to fire two or three times faster than a muzzle-loaded carbine or rifle.

[31] Symonds, p. 71; Coddington, p. 266; Eicher, pp. 510–511.

[32] Tucker, pp. 112–117.

[33] Foote, p. 468

[34] Tucker, p. 184; Symonds, p. 74; Pfanz, *First Day*, pp. 269–275.

[35] Busey and Martin, pp. 298, 501.

[36] Pfanz, *First Day*, pp. 275–293.

[37] Clark, p. 53.

[38] Pfanz, *First Day*, p. 158.

[39] Pfanz, *First Day*, p. 230.

[40] Pfanz, *First Day*, pp. 156–238.

[41] Pfanz, *First Day*, p. 294.

[42] Pfanz, *First Day*, pp. 337–338; Sears, pp. 223–225.

[43] Martin, pp. 482–488.

[44] Pfanz, *First Day*, p. 344; Eicher, p. 517; Sears, p. 228; Trudeau, p. 253. Both Sears and Trudeau record "if possible."

[45] Martin, p. 9, citing Thomas L. Livermore's *Numbers & Losses in the Civil War in America* (Houghton Mifflin, 1900).

[46] Longstreet, From Manassas to Appomattox: Memoirs of the Civil War in America, (Philadelphia:J. B. Lippincott, 1896), pp. 364, 365

[47] Clark, p. 74; Eicher, p. 521.

[48] James Longstreet, From Manassas to Appomattox. (Philadelphia, PA: J. R. Lippincott company, 1896), p. 365.

[49] Sears, p. 255; Clark, p. 69.

[50] Edward Porter Alexander, Military Memoirs of a Confederate. (New York: Charles Scribner & Sons, 1907), p. 408

[51] Longstreet, From Manassas to Appomattox: Memoirs of the Civil War in America, (Philadelphia:J. B. Lippincott, 1896), pp. 364, 368

[52] Longstreet, From Manassas to Appomattox: Memoirs of the Civil War in America, (Philadelphia:J. B. Lippincott, 1896), p. 365

[53] Longstreet, From Mannassas to Appomattox: Memoirs of the Civil War in America, p. 366

[54] Pfanz, *Second Day*, pp. 119–123.

[55] Pfanz, *Second Day*, pp. 93–97; Eicher, pp. 523–524.

[56] Longstreet, From Manassas to Appomattox: Memoirs of the Civil War in America, p. 369

[57] Eicher

[58] Harman, p. 59.

[59] Harman, p. 57.

[60] Sears, pp. 312–324; Eicher, pp. 530–535; Coddington, p. 423.

[61] Eicher, pp. 527–530; Clark, pp. 81–85.

[62] Edward Porter Alexander, Military Memoirs of a Confederate. (New York: Charles Scribner & Sons, 1907), p. 409

[63] Eicher, pp. 537–538; Sauers, p. 835; Pfanz, *Culp's Hill*, pp. 205–234; Clark, pp. 115–116.

[64] Report of Maj. Gen. R. E. Rodes, CSA, commanding division. JUNE 3-AUGUST 1, 1863.–The Gettysburg Campaign. O.R.– SERIES I–VOLUME XXVII/2 [S# 44]

[65] Sears, p. 257; Longacre, pp. 198–199.

[66] Harman, p. 63.

[67] Pfanz, *Culp's Hill*, pp. 284–352; Eicher, pp. 540–541; Coddington, pp. 465–475.

[68] Eicher, p. 542; Coddington, pp. 485–486.

[69] Longstreet, From Manassas to Appomattox: Memoirs of the Civil War in America, (Philadelphia:J. B. Lippincott, 1896), pp. 386–387

[70] See discussion of varying gun estimates in Pickett's Charge article footnote.

[71] McPherson, pp. 661–663; Clark, pp. 133–144; Symonds, pp. 214–241; Eicher, pp. 543–549.

[72] Eicher, pp. 549–550; Longacre, pp. 226–231, 240–44; Sauers, p. 836; Wert, pp. 272–280.

[73] https://www.historynet.com/gettysburg-casualties

[74] Examples of the varying Confederate casualties for July 1–3 are Sears, p. 498 (22,625); Coddington, p. 536 (20,451, "and very likely more"); Trudeau, p. 529 (22,874); Eicher, p. 550 (22,874, "but probably actually totaled 28,000 or more"); McPherson, p. 664 (28,000); Esposito, map 99 ("near 28,000"); Clark, p. 150 (20,448, "but probably closer to 28,000," which he inaccurately cites as a nearly 40% loss); Woodworth, p. 209 ("at least equal to Meade's and possibly as high as 28,000"); NPS https://web.archive.org/web/20110513133710/http://www.nps.gov/history/hps/abpp/battles/pa002.htm (28,000)

[75] Glatthaar, p. 282.

[76] Sears, p. 513.

[77] Busey and Martin, pp. 125–147, 260–315. Headquarters element casualties account for the minor differences in army totals stated previously.

[78] Catton, p. 325.

[79] Sears, p. 391.

[80] Sears, p. 511.

[81] Woodworth, p. 216.

[82] Eicher, p. 550; Coddington, pp. 539–544; Clark, pp. 146–147; Sears, p. 469; Wert, p. 300.

[83] Clark, pp. 147–157; Longacre, pp. 268–269.

[84] Coddington, p. 564.

[85] https://www.history.com/topics/american-civil-war/draft-riots

[86] Coddington, pp. 535–574; Sears, pp. 496–497; Eicher, p. 596; Wittenberg et al., *One Continuous Fight*, pp. 345–346..

[87] McPherson, p. 664.

[88] Donald, p. 446; Woodworth, p. 217.

[89] Coddington, p. 573.

[90] McPherson, pp. 650, 664.

[91] Gallagher, *Lee and His Army*, pp. 86, 93, 102–05; Sears, pp. 501–502; McPherson, p. 665, in contrast to Gallagher, depicts Lee as "profoundly depressed" about the battle.

[92] Gallagher, *Lee and His Generals*, pp. 207–208; Sears, p. 503; Woodworth, p. 221. Gallagher's essay "Jubal A. Early, The Lost Cause, and Civil War History: A Persistent Legacy" in *Lee and His Generals* is a good overview of the Lost Cause movement.

[93] White, p. 251. White refers to Lincoln's use of the term "new birth of freedom" and writes, "The *new birth* that slowly emerged in Lincoln's politics meant that on November 19 at Gettysburg he was no longer, as in his inaugural address, defending an old Union but proclaiming a new Union. The old Union contained and attempted to restrain slavery. The new Union would fulfill the promise of liberty, the crucial step into the future that the Founders had failed to take."

[94] McPherson, p. 665; Gallagher, *Lee and His Generals*, pp. 207–208.

[95] Catton, p. 331.

[96] Eicher, p. 550; McPherson, p. 665

[97] Hattaway and Jones, p. 415; Woodworth, p. xiii; Coddington, p. 573; Glatthaar, p. 288; Bearss, p. 202.

[98] Carmichael, p. xvii;

[99] Keegan, pp. 202, 239.

[100] Sears, pp. 499–500; Glatthaar, p. 287; Fuller, p. 198, states that Lee's "overweening confidence in the superiority of his soldiers over his enemy possessed him."

[101] For example, Sears, p. 504: "In the final analysis, it was Robert E. Lee's inability to manage his generals that went to the heart of the failed campaign." Glatthaar, pp. 285–286, criticizes the inability of the generals to coordinate their actions as a whole. Fuller, p. 198, states that Lee "maintained no grip over the operations" of his army.

[102] Fuller, p. 195, for example, refers to orders to Stuart that "were as usual vague." Fuller, p. 197, wrote "As was [Lee's] custom, he relied on verbal instructions, and left all details to his subordinates."

[103] Woodworth, pp. 209–210.

[104] Sears, pp. 501–502; McPherson, pp. 656–657; Coddington, pp. 375–380; A more detailed collection of historical assessments of Longstreet at Gettysburg may be found in James Longstreet#Gettysburg.

[105] Sears, p. 502; A more detailed collection of historical assessments of Stuart in the Gettysburg Campaign may be found in J.E.B. Stuart#Gettysburg.

[106] McPherson, p. 654; Coddington, pp. 317–319; Eicher, pp. 517–518; Sears, p. 503.

[107] Sears, pp. 502–503.

[108] Sears, p. 500.

[109] Sears, p. 506; Coddington, p. 573.

[110] Sears, pp. 505–507.

[111] http://home.nps.gov/gett/index.htm

[112] *Gettysburg casino plan defeated*, Penn State Civil War History Center, April 15, 2011 http://www.psu.edu/dept/richardscenter/2011/04/gettysburg-casino-plan-defeated.html

[113] https://www.battlefields.org/preserve/saved-land American Battlefield Trust "Saved Land" webpage. Accessed May 24, 2018.

[114] https://www.washingtonpost.com/news/house-divided/wp/2016/09/15/lees-gettysburg-headquarters-restored-set-to-open-oct-28/ The Washington Post, "Lee's Gettysburg headquarters restored, set to open Oct. 28." Accessed May 24, 2018.

[115] https://www.worldcat.org/oclc/5890637

[116] https://archive.is/20121215152320/http://www.dean.usma.edu/departments/history/Atlases/AmericanCivilWar/AmericanCivilWar.html

[117] https://books.google.com/books?id=xAPLeOrCoOsC&printsec=frontcover

[118] //www.worldcat.org/oclc/44957745

[119] https://web.archive.org/web/20141022014655/http://www.rocemabra.com/~roger/tagg/generals/

[120] https://books.google.com/books?id=woP8IV7zHGwC

[121] https://archive.org/details/finalreportongettys01burgrich

[122] https://www.worldcat.org/oclc/607395975

[123] http://ebooks.library.cornell.edu/m/moawar/waro.html

[124] http://www.gettysburgphotographs.com/

[125] https://www.battlefields.org/battlefields/gettysburg.html

[126] http://www.gettysburg.edu/library/gettdigital/civil_war/civilwar.htm

[127] http://www.civilwaranimated.com/GettysburgAnimation.html

[128] http://babel.hathitrust.org/cgi/pt?id=uc1.b3111589

[129] https://www.worldcat.org/oclc/4637523

[130] http://www.history.army.mil/StaffRide/Gettysburg/gettysburg_2010.pdf

[131] https://www.worldcat.org/oclc/42908450

[132] https://www.worldcat.org/oclc/22643644

[133] https://www.battlefields.org/battlefields/gettysburg/maps/gettysburg-devils-den-and.html

[134] https://www.battlefields.org/battlefields/gettysburg/maps/gettysburg-animated-map/

[135] http://www.nps.gov/gett/

[136] https://web.archive.org/web/20120304063040/http://www.nps.gov/history/history/online_books/gett/gettysburg_seminars/index.htm

[137] http://www.army.mil/gettysburg

[138] http://www.militaryhistoryonline.com/gettysburg/

[139] http://www.civilwarhome.com/gettysbu.html

[140] https://web.archive.org/web/20040926103045/http://brotherswar.com/

[141] http://www.gdg.org/

[142] http://www.bklyn-genealogy-info.com/Military/ConfederateGenerals.html

[143] http://www.britannica.com/event/Battle-of-Gettysburg

[144] https://web.archive.org/web/20110513133710/http://www.nps.gov/history/hps/abpp/battles/pa002.htm

[145] https://archive.org/details/1938-07-04_Blue_and_Gray_At_75th_Anniversary_Of_Great_Battle

[146] Eicher, pp. 450-51.

[147] Reynolds family genealogy http://library.fandm.edu/archives/Reynolds/genealogy.pdf.

[148] Warner, p. 396.

[149] Eicher, p. 450; Carney, p. 1631.

[150] Carney, p. 1632; Bearss, p. 161; Tagg, pp. 10-11.

[151] Carney, p. 1632.

[152] Carney, p. 1632; Tagg, p. 10.

[153] Sears, *To the Gates of Richmond*, p. 252.

[154] Eicher, p. 451.

[155] Tagg, p. 10.

[156] Eicher, p. 704.

[157] Sears, *Chancellorsville*, pp. 228-29, 243, 420-22; Tagg, p. 11; Carney, p. 1633; Welcher, p. 667.

[158] Sears, *Gettysburg*, pp. 40-41; Tagg, p. 11. Eicher, pp. 773-74: Although Reynolds and Meade were both promoted to major general of volunteers with the date of rank of November 29, 1862, Reynolds' name appeared immediately before Meade's on the promotion list, ranking 49th of all the volunteer major generals. After Meade's promotion, Reynolds was the third most senior corps commander in the Army of the Potomac, after Henry W. Slocum and John Sedgwick.

[159] Sources differ as to the location of the wound. Sears, *Gettysburg*, p. 170, quotes orderly Sgt. Charles S. Veil that a "Minnie ball struck him in the back of the neck." Tagg, p. 12, and Coddington, p. 269, assert the wound was behind the right ear.

[160] Trudeau, p. 271.

[161] Tagg, p. 9.

[162] Foote, p. 468.

[163] Sears, *Gettysburg*, pp. 154-225.

[164] Hawthorne, pp. 19, 82, 135.

[165] Bearss, p. 161.

[166] Sanders, pp. 27-36; Catton, 273-74; Tucker, pp. 110-11; Coddington, pp. 269, 686; Pfanz, pp. 77-78.

[167] http://www.rocemabra.com/~roger/tagg/generals/

[168] http://library.fandm.edu/archives/Reynolds/genealogy.pdf

[169] https//archive.org

[170] https://www.findagrave.com/memorial/2754

[171] http://library.fandm.edu/archives/Reynolds/JFR/scrapbook.html

[172] http://www.cclibraries.com/local_history/MexicanWar/reynoldsjf.htm

[173] http://www.artglenn.com/family/reynolds/admreynolds.htm

[174] https://archive.org/stream/barksdalefamilyh00bark/barksdalefamilyh00bark_djvu.txt

[175] Warner, p. 16.

[176] Clark, p. 102.

[177] Pfanz, pp. 320-21.

[178] William Barksdale biography http://www.genbarksdale.org/William%20Barksdale.html , Sons of Confederate Veterans.

[179] https://web.archive.org/web/20141022014655/http://www.rocemabra.com/~roger/tagg/generals/

[180] http://bioguide.congress.gov/scripts/biodisplay.pl?index=B000147

[181] https://mississippiconfederates.wordpress.com/2013/10/20/his-gallant-spirit-went-home-the-burial-of-general-william-barksdale-in-jackson/

[182] Tagg, p. 326, quoting Robert E. Lee.

[183] Wills, pp. 7–10.

[184] Wills, pp. 19, 20.

[185] Official Records, Series I, Vol. XXV, Part II, Chap. XXXVII, p. 811 http://ebooks.library.cornell.edu/cgi/t/text/pageviewer-idx?c=moawar&cc=moawar&idno=waro0040&node=waro0040%3A5&view=image&seq=813&size=100

[186] Tagg, p. 327; Eicher, p. 424.

[187] Official Records, Series I, Vol. XXVII, Part II, Chap. XXXIX, p. 325 http://ebooks.library.cornell.edu/cgi/t/text/pageviewer-idx?c=moawar;cc=moawar;idno=waro0044;node=waro0044%3A5;view=image;seq=327;size=100;page=root

[188]Official Records, Series I, Vol. XXVII, Part II, Chap. XXXIX, p. 608 http://ebooks.library.
cornell.edu/cgi/t/text/pageviewer-idx?c=moawar;cc=moawar;idno=waro0044;node=
waro0044%3A5;view=image;seq=610;size=100;page=root

[189]http://www.rocemabra.com/~roger/tagg/generals/

[190]http://ehistory.osu.edu/osu/sources/records/list.cfm

[191]https://www.findagrave.com/memorial/11048

[192]http://www.lib.unc.edu/mss/inv/p/Pender,William_Dorsey.html

[193]Smith, p. 337

[194]Smith, p. 337

[195]Smith, p. 337

[196]David Keehn, *Knights of the Golden Circle* https//books.google.com

[197]Smith, p. 337

[198]http://www.gilderlehrman.org/history-by-era/american-civil-war/resources/death-soldier-
1863-paul-semmes

[199]https://archive.org/search.php?query=publisher%3A%22Confederate%20Pub.%20Co.%22

[200]https://www.worldcat.org/oclc/833588

[201]https://www.findagrave.com/memorial/7947

[202]http://lcweb2.loc.gov/diglib/ihas/loc.natlib.ihas.200001842/pageturner.html

[203]http://sites.google.com/a/columbusstate.edu/dr-gardiner-s-course-materials/paul-semmes-
burial

[204]Eicher, p. 614, states that the appointment to brigadier general was not confirmed by the Senate.
Warner, p. 548, does not make this distinction.

[205]Report of the Secretary of War, 1860, pages 94-95 https://babel.hathitrust.org/cgi/pt?id=iau.
31858029293226;view=1up;seq=102

[206]*At Gettysburg, or, What a Girl Saw and Heard of the Battle. A True Narrative.* http://digital.
library.upenn.edu/women/alleman/gettysburg/gettysburg.html by Mrs. Matilda "Tillie" Pierce
Alleman (1848-1914). New York, W. Lake Borland, 1889.

[207]http://digital.library.upenn.edu/women/alleman/gettysburg/gettysburg.html

[208]https://www.findagrave.com/memorial/6142

[209]The Grand Army of the Republic: Bean's 1884 History of Montgomery County, Pennsylvania
http://files.usgwarchives.org/pa/montgomery/history/local/mchb0022.txt

[210]Warner, p. 576.

[211]Eide, Bradley, Gettysburg Discussion Group biography http://www.gdg.org/Research/OOB/
Union/July1-3/szook.html

[212]Eicher, p. 586.

[213]Warner, p. 577.

[214]*Virtual Gettysburg* http://www.virtualgettysburg.com/exhibit/monuments/pages/cm059.html

[215]New York (State) et al., p. 421.

[216]https://books.google.com/books?id=rQUTAAAAYAAJ

[217]https://www.worldcat.org/oclc/607395975

[218]https://web.archive.org/web/20141022014655/http://www.rocemabra.com/~roger/tagg/
generals/

[219]Wright, p. 179, describes this name as "a joke on the shy and quiet-spoken widower who was
known to admire the ladies." Foote, pp. 533-34, writes "A widower ... he was a great admirer
of the ladies and enjoyed posing as a swain. This had earned him the nickname 'Lo,' an abbrevi-
ation Lothario, which was scarcely in keeping with his close-cropped, grizzled beard or receding
hairline.

[220]Armistead, lewis addison (1817-1863). Encyclopedia of the American Civil War: A Political,
Social, and Military History. 2000.

[221]The Armistead Family: 1635-1910 By Virginia Armistead Garber pg. 15

[222]Encyclopedia Smithsonian: Star Spangled Banner and the War of 1812: http://www.si.edu/
encyclopedia_Si/nmah/starflag.htm Making the Star Spangled Banner

[223]*Resignation of Cadet Lewis A. Armistead*, January 29, 1836, RG 77, E 18, National Archives.
Eicher, p. 107, states that he "resigned presumably" for breaking the plate. Wert, p. 40, and
Warner, p. 11, characterize Armistead as being "dismissed" from the Academy for his action.

Poindexter, p. 144 (the source credited by Warner), recalls that Armistead "was retired from West Point."

[224] Johnson, p. 78.

[225] Krick, pp. 104-05. Krick, one of the foremost historians of the Army of Northern Virginia, does not acknowledge multiple marriages. He states that Cecilia (his spelling) died on August 3, 1855, at Fort Riley, Kansas, during a cholera epidemic.

[226] Eicher, p. 107.

[227] Krick, p. 110; "The Native Americans of Joshua Tree National Park: An Ethnographic Overview and Assessment Study/" http://www.nps.gov/history/history/online_books/jotr/history7.htm Cultural Systems Research, Inc., August 22, 2002, VII. Mojave.

[228] Krick, p. 110.

[229] Halleran, Michael A. *The Better Angels of Our Nature: Freemasonry in the American Civil War*. Tuscaloosa: The University of Alabama Press, 2010. pp. 26–30

[230] *Armistead's Death* http://www.gdg.org/Research/People/Armistead/dtarm.html, article at Gettysburg Discussion Group by Bryan Meyer.

[231] Henry Bishop, Sr. sold the property in 1848 to George Spangler. At the time of the sale the farm consisted of some 80 acres. Spangler lived on the property for fifty-six years and died in his 88th year in the home in 1904.

[232] Smith, pp. 174-75.

[233] Poindexter, pp. 144, 150.

[234] http://www.rocemabra.com/~roger/tagg/generals/

[235] http://www.gdg.org/Research/People/Armistead/dtarm.html

[236] http://encyclopediavirginia.org/Armistead_Lewis_A_1817-1863

[237] https://www.findagrave.com/memorial/3493

[238] http://uknet.com/armisteads/Confederate-Veteran--Nov-1914/

[239] Eicher, John H., and David J. Eicher. *Civil War High Commands*. Stanford, CA: Stanford University Press, 2001. p. 596.

[240] Petruzzi, J. David, "Elon J. Farnsworth" http://petruzzi.wordpress.com/2007/06/13/faded-hoofbeats-elon-j-farnsworth/, *Faded Hoofbeats* blog, June 13, 2007.

[241] Wert, Jeffry D. *Gettysburg: Day Three*. New York: Simon & Schuster, 2001. p. 278: "Subsequent accounts by Confederates alleging that he had committed suicide are bogus."

[242] https://www.findagrave.com/memorial/5842062

[243] https://en.wikisource.org/wiki/Appletons%27_Cyclop%C3%A6dia_of_American_Biography/Farnsworth,_John_Franklin

[244] Eicher, p. 249.

[245] Dozier, Graham T. Richard B. Garnett (1817–1863) http://www.encyclopediavirginia.org/garnett_richard_b_1817-1863#start_entry *Encyclopedia Virginia*. Web. 9 March 2016.

[246] Wert, p. 287.

[247] Krick, p. 122; Wert, p. 213; Hess, p. 265; Eicher, p. 249: Cause of death was possibly due to being "... hit in the head, Gettysburg, Pa., July 3, 1863."

[248] Possible confirmation from Union sources: In *Battles and Leaders of the Civil War* Vol 3, p. 388, Lt. Col. Edmund Rice of the 19th Massachusetts reported that in front of his line of the 19th Massachusetts and 42nd New York, '... I saw one leader several times try to jump his horse over our line. He was shot by some of the men near me ...". The Gettysburg Cyclorama mistakenly shows General Armistead falling mortally wounded from his horse near the Union lines—he was actually afoot. If this painting was based on Rice's report, the Confederate officer falling from his horse was actually Garnett.

[249] Hess, p. 265: the horse was seen racing to the rear with a severe wound. Krick, p. 122: the horse was badly wounded along with Garnett and could not move, citing an account by Lt. Col. Norborne Berkeley of Garnett's Brigade. In the 1993 film *Gettysburg*, his horse is portrayed running riderless to the rear.

[250] E. Porter Alexander in *Battles and Leaders of the Civil War* Vol 3, p. 365, reported that Garnett had come out of an ambulance to lead his brigade in Pickett's Charge and was "... buttoned up in an old blue overcoat ..."

[251] Krick, p. 123.

[252] Wert, pp. 291-93. Armistead died of his wounds on July 5. Kemper was wounded, captured by Union troops, and then rescued by the Confederates and returned to Virginia.

[253] Eicher, pp. 249-50.

[254] Krick, p. 96.

[255] Garnett, Doug, "Hidden at the National Archives", *America's Civil War*, September 2009, p. 6.

[256] https://web.archive.org/web/20080208215607/http://www.generalsandbrevets.com/sgd/daniel.htm

[257] http://encyclopediavirginia.org/Garnett_Richard_B_1817-1863

[258] https://web.archive.org/web/20030507160612/http://www.stonewall.hut.ru/leaders/garnett.htm

[259] Tagg, p. 343.

[260] Hess, pp. 38-40.

[261] Busey & Martin, p. 286.

[262] Gottfried, p. 606.

[263] Official Records, Series 1, Vol. 27, Part 3, page 1016.

[264] http://www.rocemabra.com/~roger/tagg/generals/

[265] http://ehistory.osu.edu/osu/sources/records/list.cfm

[266] //lccn.loc.gov/59-8864

[267] https://archive.org/details/memorialoflifeof00tres

[268] https://www.worldcat.org/oclc/3557938

[269] https://www.findagrave.com/memorial/11050

[270] http://www.nps.gov/gett/getttour/tstops/tstd3-21jjp.htm

[271] http://www.ncparks.gov/Visit/parks/pett/history.php

[272] https://web.archive.org/web/20080208215607/http://www.generalsandbrevets.com/sgp/petti.htm

[273] https://archive.org/stream/confederatememor03ladi

[274] Eicher, p. 614.

[275] Norton, p. 167. Norton was a member of the 83rd Pennsylvania, which Vincent commanded before becoming its brigade commander.

[276] Warner, p. 528. Eicher, p. 614, states that this promotion was not confirmed by the United States Senate, and therefore does not list him as a general.

[277] Norton, p. 162.

[278] https://web.archive.org/web/20050411174515/http://www.vincent.goellnitz.org/

[279] https://archive.org/details/armyletters1861100nort

[280] https://www.worldcat.org/oclc/24611059

[281] https://books.google.com/books?id=KmiDAl1_byUC

Article Sources and Contributors

The sources listed for each article provide more detailed licensing information including the copyright status, the copyright owner, and the license conditions.

Battle of Gettysburg *Source:* https://en.wikipedia.org/w/index.php?oldid=927472900 *License:* Creative Commons Attribution-Share Alike 3.0 *Contributors:* A D Monroe III, Acroterion, Adam Cuerden, Arjayay, Audaciter, Auric, Banedon, Bender235, Berean Hunter, Berty688, Bgwhite, Bigturtle, Brandmeister, Bright Darkness, Bulls123, BusterD, Capt Jim, Central Data Bank, Chainclaw, ChrisGualtieri, Clarityfiend, Cobaltcigs, Coltsfan, Dagos-Navy, Darthkenobi0, David Koller, DavisGL, DeVerm, DemonKyoto, Dinkytown, Display name 99, Dissident, Djkeddie, DocWatson42, Donaldecoho, Doncram, Donner60, Dristarg, Dsk korona, Eight nation alliance fan102, Erik L'Ensle, EyeTruth, FDRMRZUSA, Flconn, Frietjes, Funkquake, Future-Trillionaire, GELongstreet, Gaius Cornelius, GenQuest, Georgie lennon8705, Gillywell, Glacier109, Grapestomper9, Green Giant, GreenC, Greendevil32, GusF, Gwillhickers, Hamiltondaniel, HandsomeFella, Hbdragon88, HeartSpeaker, Hlj, Hmains, Ibadibam, IcarusPhoenix, Illegitimate Barrister, Iseult, It Is Me Here, Italia2006, J 1982, J. 'mach' wust, JJonahJackalope, Jabberjaw, JamesA, Jauerback, Javert2113, Jim1138, Jojhutton, Jonathan Markoff, Jonesey95, Joshmaul, Jperrylsu, Jusdafax, KConWiki, Kh80, Khazar2, Kobrabones, Krazytea, LFevas, Laodah, Ledfrog, LeoFrank, Liberty823, Lieutco-luseng, LightandDark2000, LilHelpa, Look2See1, Lswiader, Mabuhay92, Maczkopeti, Madalino, Mandruss, Materialscientist, MatthewJ00, MeanMotherJr, Mickey Featherstone, Molly-in-md, Monochrome Monitor, Mortense, Mrhalohunter24, Msclguru, Niceguyedc, Nick Moyes, Nickrulercreator, Nihiltres, Old timer1776, PeacePeace, Pedro8790, Petronius2, Powerfuller, Prestonmag, ProudIrishAspie, R. S. Shaw, Randy Kryn, Re34646, Red Director, Rich Farm-brough, Rivertorch, RjCan, Rumiton, SCRebel1740, Satellizer, SaveOurHistory, Scriblerian1, Seraphimblade, SergeantHippyZombie, Shyjayb, Snorvege, Somakip, SpikeToronto, StaedtlerTheOnLy, Stefan97, Stevietheman, StjJackson, Strebe, Sundayclose, Tassedethe, The PIPE, TheVirginiaHistorian, The-hornet, Tigerboy1966, Tobby72, Tom, Tomandjerry211, TypoBoy, USNorseman, Valetude, WP Ludicer, Werieth, Wikid77, Wjcfreelancer, WolfmanSF, Ycleymans, Yorkshiremany, Zackmann08, Zedshort, Zppix, 展翅飛翔 7

John F. Reynolds *Source:* https://en.wikipedia.org/w/index.php?oldid=926554824 *License:* Creative Commons Attribution-Share Alike 3.0 *Contrib-utors:* 4A1E0S, 8th Ohio Volunteers, Aboutmovies, AjGAMER10145, AndarielHalo, Awilley, BD2412, Baa, Bkwillwm, Bobo192, BrownHairedGirl, BusterD, Caltrop, CaroleHenson, Catgut, CivilWarReenactor1863, Closedmouth, ClueBot NG, Connormah, Corlier, Crystallizedcarbon, D6, Danvera, Di-annaa, Display name 99, Dissident, Doncram, Donner60, EWikist, Eeekster, Elendil's Heir, Fdewaele, Flyer22 Reborn, Francvs, Fyyer, GabeHanafin, Gildir, Gilliam, Good Olfactory, Graeme Cook, GreenC, HJ Mitchell, HennessyC, HenryLi, Hlj, Hmains, Howcheng, HuoYuanjia10, I dream of horses, Ibadibam, Illegitimate Barrister, JJMC89, Jaraalbe, Jdaloner, Jovianeye, Jujutacular, Julius.kusuma, Jwillbur, Katalaveno, Kbuddha420, Kenatipo, King of Hearts, Kingwhick, Kittybrewster, Kresock, Kumioko (renamed), LA2, Labant, Looper5920, MK2, MadeYourReadThis, Magioladitis, Marechal Ney, Mark Arsten, Michael David, Mike Selinker, Mrmdog, NCDane, NickBradford1, North Shoreman, NuclearWarfare, OG Aramis, Passionless, Pats1, Piled-higheranddeeper, Ppoison287, ProudIrishAspie, Pubdog, RWReagan, Rich Farmbrough, Rlevse, RobotG, Ryuhaku, Scalasaig, Scott Mingus, Sct72, SeanO, Ser Amantio di Nicolao, SheepNotGoats, SimonP, Skwiid, Slante9, Spacini, Susvolans, Tabletop, The Mystery Man, The wub, Tide rolls, Ugen64, Widr, Woohookitty, Wwoods, YellowMonkey, Yukisealive, BoenTex, 119 anonymous edits 59

William Barksdale *Source:* https://en.wikipedia.org/w/index.php?oldid=922795304 *License:* Creative Commons Attribution-Share Alike 3.0 *Contrib-utors:* 2112 rush, 8th Ohio Volunteers, Aboutmovies, Agathman, Americus55, Animalparty, BusterD, CWenger, Cabayi, CommonsDelinker, Dave Dial, Daysleeper47, De132Wiki, Deisenbe, Donald Albury, Donner60, Drmies, Dsdugan, Egghamsale, F McGady, Florian Huber, FourthAve, GELongstreet, GeoWPC, Good Olfactory, GrahamHardy, GünniX, Hlj, Hmains, JJMC89, JimmyJoe87, Joshmaul, Jprg1966, Jwillbur, Kingwhick, Kumioko (renamed), Leeannbarksdalebartel, Lekoren, Lockley, Micheal napoier, Mickey Featherstone, Mjdejong, Niceguyedc, Prof .Woodruff, ProudIrishAspie, R'n'B, Rich Farmbrough, RobotG, SDriskell, Scott Mingus, Seelowe33, Ser Amantio di Nicolao, SideKick94, Sjö, StjJackson, The wub, Thismightbezach, Turgan, Velocicaptor, Woodlot, Woohookitty, 53 anonymous edits 71

William Dorsey Pender *Source:* https://en.wikipedia.org/w/index.php?oldid=915742580 *License:* Creative Commons Attribution-Share Alike 3.0 *Contributors:* 248Garland, BOTijo, Bamyers99, Bluemoose, CWenger, CommonsDelinker, CutOffTies, Deville, Donner60, Fdewaele, GELongstreet, Gilliam, Hlj, Hmains, JJMC89, Kges1901, Khan singh, Kingwhick, Kitt1987, Klemen Kocjancic, Kumioko (renamed), Looper5920, Lordbowler, Mickey Featherstone, Monegasque, Postdlf, ProudIrishAspie, Pubdog, Ravensworth, Rich Farmbrough, RobotG, Scott Mingus, StjJackson, The wub, Timwest02, TomIzbick, Valetude, Wwoods, 14 anonymous edits 77

Paul Jones Semmes *Source:* https://en.wikipedia.org/w/index.php?oldid=882991393 *License:* Creative Commons Attribution-Share Alike 3.0 *Con-tributors:* Bearcat, Bender235, CommonsDelinker, Donner60, Faizan, Gjs238, Gspurloc, Hilltoppers, Hlj, Hmains, Jehorn, Jwillbur, Kingwhick, Klemen Kocjancic, Kumioko (renamed), Lekoren, Magioladitis, Maxrossomachin, Pi3.124, ProudIrishAspie, RobotG, Scott Mingus, Steevo714, TAnthony, The wub, Waacstats, Xezbeth, Basil, 5 anonymous edits 82

Stephen H. Weed *Source:* https://en.wikipedia.org/w/index.php?oldid=927265834 *License:* Creative Commons Attribution-Share Alike 3.0 *Contrib-utors:* BD2412, BOTijo, Cacrats, Davehi1, Dkennert, Donner60, Drmies, Fdewaele, Haus, Hilltoppers, Hlj, Hmains, Illegitimate Barrister, JJMC89, Kumioko (renamed), LiamKasbar, Mary Mark Ockerbloom, Mickey Featherstone, Mike Selinker, Nicholasweed, Old Scarecrow, ProudIrishAspie, Rich Farmbrough, RobDuch, RobotG, Ronhjones, Saga City, Scewing, Scott Mingus, Searcher 1990, Spacini, Station1, The wub, TheAllknowingMuffelbuns, WikiDan61, 9 anonymous edits 85

Samuel K. Zook *Source:* https://en.wikipedia.org/w/index.php?oldid=918202425 *License:* Creative Commons Attribution-Share Alike 3.0 *Contrib-utors:* 1ForTheMoney, 8th Ohio Volunteers, Bender235, Bob Burkhardt, Bobo192, BoringHistoryGuy, BusterD, Circeus, ClueBot NG, Col-ibri37, Donner60, Drmies, Fdewaele, GELongstreet, GreenMeansGo, Historygeek2044, Hlj, Hmains, I dream of horses, Illegitimate Barrister, JJMC89, Kingwhick, Klemen Kocjancic, Kumioko (renamed), LibLord, Ligulem, Mac3387, MadMax, Mets501, Micael jackson is turd, Mickey Featherstone, Mike Selinker, OccultZone, PBS-AWB, Planetguy, ProudIrishAspie, Rich Farmbrough, RobotG, Scott Mingus, Sitethief, Spacini, Startstop123, The Mystery Man, The wub, TiMike, Tom.Reding, Wiley G, 20 anonymous edits 88

Lewis Armistead *Source:* https://en.wikipedia.org/w/index.php?oldid=924636861 *License:* Creative Commons Attribution-Share Alike 3.0 *Contrib-utors:* $1LENCE D00600D, 1990'sguy, 1ForTheMoney, 248Garland, Aboutmovies, Accurizer, Amcfreely, Arthur Ellis, Asadron, Ashley Pomeroy, Asiaticus, Auntieruth55, Barnej, Bedford, Berean Hunter, Bilsonius, Biruitorul, Blueboar, Can't sleep, clown will eat me, Capricorn42, Cethomas1234, Chicheley, ChrisGualtieri, Cloonmore, ClueBot NG, CommonsDelinker, Damslerset, Deb, Display name 99, Donner60, Econrad, Edward, Eight-Nation-Alliance fan101, Elpe, Evenrød, FourthAve, Fred26, Fredrik, GABaker, GDW13, GELongstreet, Gallifrey102, GoingBatty, Goltz20707, Hilltoppers, Hlj, Hmains, Iconoclast.horizon, JJMC89, Jadewik, JamesAM, JazzD, Jmboothe, Jordan 1972, Joshmaul, Jprg1966, Jwillbur, KConWiki, Kbseah, Keith D, Kilo-Lima, Kingwhick, Kitt1987, Klemen Kocjancic, Kresock, Kumioko (renamed), Kyle122802, Lawrie, Lekoren, Lotje, Lowercase Sigma, MAJArkay, Magic Lemur, Mambo Bananapatch, Margo&Gladys, MatthewSMaynard, MayerG, Millhouse1990, Monegasque, Niceguyedc, Nn123645, Npeters22, NuclearWarfare, Omfreakinggoodness, Onel5969, Piledhigheranddeeper, ProudIrishAspie, Psdubow, Rklear, Rlevse, Rms125a@hotmail.com, RobotG, Ronzzo, Ryuhaku, Sand Emu, Scott Mingus, Sherurcij, SimonP, SongspiritUSA, Stevelance, StjJackson, TeriEmbrey, The Frog, The Mystery Man, The wub, Tide rolls, Ulric1313, Valetude, VoABot II, WOSlinker, Wikidicki4, Wmcewenjr, Woohookitty, Wsandoval443, Yamamoto Ichiro, 126 anonymous edits 95

Elon J. Farnsworth *Source:* https://en.wikipedia.org/w/index.php?oldid=910620892 *License:* Creative Commons Attribution-Share Alike 3.0 *Contrib-utors:* Alai, BD2412, Berean Hunter, Bluedudemi, Bob Burkhardt, CWenger, Donner60, ExtraordinaryMan, Fluffernutter, Haus, Hede2000, Hilltoppers, Hlj, Hmains, Hugh Manatee, Illegitimate Barrister, JJMC89, Johnpacklambert, Kevin B12, Kingwhick, Kranar drogin, Kresock, Kumioko (renamed), Mickey Featherstone, Mike Selinker, Nikkimaria, PBS-AWB, ProudIrishAspie, R'n'B, Rich Farmbrough, Richard Arthur Norton (1958-), Richardawalker, RobotG, Sarcasmboy, Scott Mingus, Searcher 1990, Serols, Spacini, The wub, 21 anonymous edits 102

Richard B. Garnett *Source:* https://en.wikipedia.org/w/index.php?oldid=903502026 *License:* Creative Commons Attribution-Share Alike 3.0 *Contrib-utors:* 8th Ohio Volunteers, BOTijo, Bob Burkhardt, BusterD, CWenger, Cacrats, ClueBot NG, CommonsDelinker, Davehi1, Display name 99, Donner60, Drmies, Flyer22 Reborn, Formerly the IP-Address 24.22.227.53, Geologyguy, Hlj, Hmains, JJMC89, Joshmaul, Jprg1966, JustAGal, Jwill-bur, KConWiki, Kingwhick, Kresock, Kumioko (renamed), Lyricmac, Magioladitis, Margo&Gladys, Mickey Featherstone, Mike Selinker, MiniGamer, MisterCake, Nick, Peyre, Philkon, ProudIrishAspie, RebelAt, Rklear, Rlevse, RobotG, Rrostrom, Ryuhaku, Saxonjf, Scott Mingus, Sectryan, Snideology, Spacini, Superpenguin21, The wub, Ulric1313, Woohookitty, Yortzec, 54 anonymous edits 106

J. Johnston Pettigrew *Source:* https://en.wikipedia.org/w/index.php?oldid=925458446 *License:* Creative Commons Attribution-Share Alike 3.0 *Con-tributors:* 248Garland, 8th Ohio Volunteers, BOTijo, Bellhalla, Bender235, BrownHairedGirl, Captain-tucker, CarolinianJeff, ClueBot NG, Commons-Delinker, CutOffTies, DFW Rider, Dcirovic, Display name 99, Dole2007, Donner60, GMan552, GSS, GoneAwayNowAndRetired, Hbdragon88, Hen-nessyC, HeyItsAKnome, Hilltoppers, Hlj, Hmains, Hywel Dda, Jcbarr, Jonathan Markoff, Kingwhick, Klemen Kocjancic, Kumioko (renamed), Lekoren, Lieutcoluseng, Lpockras, MoRpH MaFiA, Monegasque, Montalban, Neier, ProudIrishAspie, Pubdog, Rnedbal, RobotG, Ryuhaku, SCRebel1740, Sam8, Scewing, Scott Mingus, Ser Amantio di Nicolao, Solar-Wind, Spoonkymonkey, StjJackson, Taneya, Taterian, The Mystery Man, The wub, TomIzbick, TonyW, Vanamonde93, Waacstats, Windypoint, WolfmanSF, Woohookitty, Yellowspacehopper, 36 anonymous edits 113

Strong Vincent *Source:* https://en.wikipedia.org/w/index.php?oldid=914046153 *License:* Creative Commons Attribution-Share Alike 3.0 *Contribu-tors:* 1ForTheMoney, BOTijo, Bender235, CWenger, Capricorn42, Chasingsol, Clarityfiend, Cornellrockey, D6, Display name 99, Donner60, Hilltop-pers, Hlj, Hmains, Illegitimate Barrister, Iridescent, JJMC89, JamesAM, JamesCivilWarT, Johnpacklambert, Joshmaul, Kingwhick, Kumioko (renamed), Looper5920, Mfields1, Michael Dorosh, Mike Selinker, Monegasque, Niagara, Pnoble805, ProudIrishAspie, RFM57, Rich Farmbrough, Robhmac, RobotG,

Image Sources, Licenses and Contributors

The sources listed for each image provide more detailed licensing information including the copyright status, the copyright owner, and the license conditions.

Image *Source:* https://en.wikipedia.org/w/index.php?title=File:Semi-protection-shackle.svg *License:* Public Domain *Contributors:* User:XYZtSpace 7

Image *Source:* https://en.wikipedia.org/w/index.php?title=File:Move-protection-shackle.svg *License:* Public Domain *Contributors:* User:XYZtSpace 7

Image *Source:* https://en.wikipedia.org/w/index.php?title=File:Thure_de_Thulstrup_-_L._Prang_and_Co._-_Battle_of_Gettysburg_-_Restoration_by_Adam_Cuerden.jpg *License:* Attribution *Contributors:* User:Adam Cuerden 7

Image *Source:* https://en.wikipedia.org/w/index.php?title=File:Flag_of_the_United_States_(1861-1863).svg *License:* Public Domain *Contributors:* Benzoyl, Cycn, Homo lupus, Illegitimate Barrister, Jacobolus, SiBr4, SpinnerLaserz, Wikiborg, Zscout370, X, 3 anonymous edits 7

Image *Source:* https://en.wikipedia.org/w/index.php?title=File:Flag_of_the_Confederate_States_of_America_(1863-1865).svg *Contributors:* - . 7

Figure 1 *Source:* https://en.wikipedia.org/w/index.php?title=File:ATLAS_OR_VIRGINIA-MARYLAND-PENNSYLVANIA.jpg *License:* Public Domain *Contributors:* FDRMRZUSA, Taterian 9

Figure 2 *Source:* https://en.wikipedia.org/w/index.php?title=File:ATLAS_OR_GETTYSBURG_CAMPAIGN_MAP.jpg *License:* Public Domain *Contributors:* FDRMRZUSA, Taterian 9

Figure 3 *Source:* https://en.wikipedia.org/w/index.php?title=File:ATLAS_OR_GETTYSBURG_BATTLEFIELD.jpg *License:* Public Domain *Contributors:* FDRMRZUSA, Jdx, Taterian, 1 anonymous edits 10

Image *Source:* https://en.wikipedia.org/w/index.php?title=File:Loudspeaker.svg *License:* Public Domain *Contributors:* Bayo, Frank C. Müller, Gmaxwell, Gnosygnu, Graphium, Husky, IagoQnsi, Iamunknown, Mirithing, Myself488, Nethac DIU, Nixón, Omegatron, Richardkiwi, Rocket000, Shanmugamp7, Snow Blizzard, Steinsplitter, Tacsipacsi, The Evil IP address, Thomas Linard, Túrelio, Wouterhagens, 31 anonymous edits 8

Figure 4 *Source:* https://en.wikipedia.org/w/index.php?title=File:Gettysburg_Campaign.png *License:* Creative Commons Attribution 3.0 *Contributors:* BotMultichill, Hlj, Ipankonin, LERK, SBaker43, Shyam 11

Figure 5 *Source:* https://en.wikipedia.org/w/index.php?title=File:FieldOfGettysburg1863.PNG *License:* Public Domain *Contributors:* Theodore Ditterline 12

Figure 6 *Source:* https://en.wikipedia.org/w/index.php?title=File:Negroes_Being_Driven_South_By_the_Rebel_Officers_(November_1862),_by_Harper's_Weekly.jpg *Contributors:* Illegitimate Barrister, WFinch, Wieralee 13

Figure 7 *Source:* https://en.wikipedia.org/w/index.php?title=File:George_G._Meade_Standing.jpg *License:* Public Domain *Contributors:* Mathew Brady (cleaned up by Hal Jespersen at en.wikipedia) 14

Figure 8 *Source:* https://en.wikipedia.org/w/index.php?title=File:GenJFRenyolds.jpg *License:* Public Domain *Contributors:* GELongstreet, MKir 13, Magog the Ogre, Mutter Erde, O (bot), Taterian 15

Figure 9 *Source:* https://en.wikipedia.org/w/index.php?title=File:WinfieldSHancock.png *License:* Public Domain *Contributors:* Finavon, FlickreviewR, Friedlibend und tapfer 15

Figure 10 *Source:* https://en.wikipedia.org/w/index.php?title=File:Daniel_Edgar_Sickles.jpg *License:* Public Domain *Contributors:* Library of Congress Prints and Photographs Division 16

Figure 11 *Source:* https://en.wikipedia.org/w/index.php?title=File:GenGS.jpg *License:* Public Domain *Contributors:* Brady National Photographic Art Gallery (Washington, D.C.) 16

Figure 12 *Source:* https://en.wikipedia.org/w/index.php?title=File:John_Sedgwick.png *License:* Public Domain *Contributors:* File Upload Bot (Magnus Manske), Fæ, Giggy, OgreBot 2, Quadell, Sfan00 IMG 17

Figure 13 *Source:* https://en.wikipedia.org/w/index.php?title=File:Oliver_Otis_Howard.jpg *License:* Public Domain *Contributors:* Mathew Brady (1823?-1896) or Levin C. Handy (1855?-1932) 17

Figure 14 *Source:* https://en.wikipedia.org/w/index.php?title=File:Henry_Warner_Slocum.jpg *License:* Public Domain *Contributors:* BrokenSphere, Fæ, MarkSweep, Mutter Erde, OsamaK, Red devil 666, Taterian 18

Figure 15 *Source:* https://en.wikipedia.org/w/index.php?title=File:Alfred_Pleasonton.jpg *License:* Public Domain *Contributors:* Calliopejen1, Ecummenic, Finavon, Fæ, Mtsmallwood, OgreBot 2 18

Figure 16 *Source:* https://en.wikipedia.org/w/index.php?title=File:Robert_Edward_Lee.jpg *Contributors:* Anathema, Apaleutos25, Blight55, Cirt, DIREKTOR, Dbenzhuser, Goldfishbutt, Jed, Makthorpe, OgreBot 2, Orionist, Rlevse, Roseohioresident, Scewing, SomeDudeWithAUserName, Taterian, Timichal, Tom, Zaccarias, 1 anonymous edits 20

Figure 17 *Source:* https://en.wikipedia.org/w/index.php?title=File:James_Longstreet.jpg *License:* Public Domain *Contributors:* Aschroet, Bob Burkhardt, BotMultichill, BotMultichillT, Illegitimate Barrister, Indefatigable2, Red devil 666, SGT141, Saforrest 20

Figure 18 *Source:* https://en.wikipedia.org/w/index.php?title=File:Richard_S_Ewell.png *License:* Public Domain *Contributors:* Library of Congress Prints and Photographs Division 21

Figure 19 *Source:* https://en.wikipedia.org/w/index.php?title=File:Image_of_Lieutenant_General_A.P._Hill.jpg *License:* Public Domain *Contributors:* User:Rlevse 21

Figure 20 *Source:* https://en.wikipedia.org/w/index.php?title=File:Jeb_stuart.jpg *Contributors:* - 22

Figure 21 *Source:* https://en.wikipedia.org/w/index.php?title=File:Gettysburg_Battle_Map_Day1.png *License:* Creative Commons Attribution 3.0 *Contributors:* BotMultichill, Botteville, Edmund Ferman, Hlj, Mtsmallwood 23

Figure 22 *Source:* https://en.wikipedia.org/w/index.php?title=File:First_shot_marker.jpg *License:* Creative Commons Attribution-Sharealike 3.0 *Contributors:* User:Lpockras 24

Figure 23 *Source:* https://en.wikipedia.org/w/index.php?title=File:Gettysburg_Day2_Plan.png *License:* Creative Commons Attribution 3.0 *Contributors:* BotMultichill, Hlj, Mtsmallwood, Rheo1905~commonswiki 26

Figure 24 *Source:* https://en.wikipedia.org/w/index.php?title=File:Gettysburg_Battle_Map_Day2.png *License:* Creative Commons Attribution 3.0 *Contributors:* BotMultichill, Hlj, Mtsmallwood, Rheo1905~commonswiki 28

Figure 25 *Source:* https://en.wikipedia.org/w/index.php?title=File:Union_breastworks_Culp's_Hill_Gettysburg.jpg *License:* Public Domain *Contributors:* Edmund Ferman, Gavin.collins, Glenn, Meteor2017 30

Figure 26 *Source:* https://en.wikipedia.org/w/index.php?title=File:Gettysburg_Battle_Map_Day3.png *License:* Creative Commons Attribution 3.0 *Contributors:* Hlj, Miroslav Cika, Mtsmallwood, OgreBot 2, 3 anonymous edits 31

Figure 27 *Source:* https://en.wikipedia.org/w/index.php?title=File:High_Water_Mark_-_Cemetery_Ridge,_Gettysburg_Battlefield.jpg *License:* Public Domain *Contributors:* Sculpture: signed Stephens.Photo: Robert Swanson (en:User:Ryssby) 33

Figure 28 *Source:* https://en.wikipedia.org/w/index.php?title=File:Battle_of_Gettysburg.jpg *Contributors:* Andrew c, Avron, BoringHistoryGuy, Choess, Christoph Braun, Ecummenic, Flominator, George Ho, Jdx, Jed, Jfire, Jpda, KAMiKAZOW, Panoptik~commonswiki, Taterian, Thuresson, Timeshifter, Wouterhagens, Yann, Zaccarias, 4 anonymous edits 35

Figure 29 *Source:* https://en.wikipedia.org/w/index.php?title=File:Gettysburg_Campaign_Retreat.png *License:* Creative Commons Attribution 3.0 *Contributors:* Drawn by Hal Jespersen in Adobe Illustrator CS5 37

Figure 30 *Source:* https://en.wikipedia.org/w/index.php?title=File:Crowd_of_citizens,_soldiers,_and_etc._with_Lincoln_at_Gettysburg._-_NARA_-_529085_-crop.jpg *License:* Public Domain *Contributors:* Scewing, Taterian 40

Figure 31 *Source:* https://en.wikipedia.org/w/index.php?title=File:Gettysburg_national_cemetery_img_4164.jpg *License:* GNU Free Documentation License *Contributors:* Photo: Henryhartley at en.wikipedia Statue: Randolph Rogers (1825-1892) 41

Figure 32 *Source:* https://en.wikipedia.org/w/index.php?title=File:George_G._Meade_Standing.jpg *License:* Public Domain *Contributors:* Mathew Brady (cleaned up by Hal Jespersen at en.wikipedia) 43

Figure 33 *Source:* https://en.wikipedia.org/w/index.php?title=File:Robert_Edward_Lee.jpg *Contributors:* Anathema, Apaleutos25, Blight55, Cirt, DIREKTOR, Dbenzhuser, Goldfishbutt, Jed, Makthorpe, OgreBot 2, Orionist, Rlevse, Roseohioresident, Scewing, SomeDudeWithAUserName, Taterian, Timichal, Tom, Zaccarias, 1 anonymous edits 44

Figure 34 *Source:* https://en.wikipedia.org/w/index.php?title=File:WinfieldSHancock.png *License:* Public Domain *Contributors:* Finavon, FlickreviewR, Friedlibend und tapfer 46

Image *Source:* https://en.wikipedia.org/w/index.php?title=File:CW_Arty_M1857_Napoleon_front.jpg *License:* Public Domain *Contributors:* Avron, Bukvoed, Chris Light, Rcbutcher, Turkmen, WBTS-Forum.de, 1 anonymous edits 47

Figure 35 *Source:* https://en.wikipedia.org/w/index.php?title=File:Battle_of_gettysburg_half_dollar_commemorative_obverse.jpg *License:* Public Domain *Contributors:* Another Believer, Searchme, Urban~commonswiki, 1 anonymous edits 49

Figure 36 *Source:* https://en.wikipedia.org/w/index.php?title=File:Gettysburg_Centennial_1963-5c.jpg *License:* Public Domain *Contributors:* Bureau of Engraving and Printing. Designed by Roy Gjertson. 49

License

143

Index

www.ingramcontent.com/pod-product-compliance
Lightning Source LLC
LaVergne TN
LVHW041318200726
843509LV00009B/544